S. Hrg. 112–203

CHINA'S ROLE IN AFRICA: IMPLICATIONS FOR U.S. POLICY

HEARING

BEFORE THE

SUBCOMMITTEE ON AFRICAN AFFAIRS

OF THE

COMMITTEE ON FOREIGN RELATIONS
UNITED STATES SENATE

ONE HUNDRED TWELFTH CONGRESS

FIRST SESSION

NOVEMBER 1, 2011

Printed for the use of the Committee on Foreign Relations

Available via the World Wide Web: http://www.gpo.gov/fdsys/

U.S. GOVERNMENT PRINTING OFFICE

72–397 PDF

WASHINGTON : 2012

For sale by the Superintendent of Documents, U.S. Government Printing Office
Internet: bookstore.gpo.gov Phone: toll free (866) 512–1800; DC area (202) 512–1800
Fax: (202) 512–2104 Mail: Stop IDCC, Washington, DC 20402–0001

(II)

CONTENTS

CHINA'S ROLE IN AFRICA: IMPLICATIONS FOR U.S. POLICY

TUESDAY, NOVEMBER 1, 2011

U.S. SENATE,
SUBCOMMITTEE ON AFRICAN AFFAIRS,
COMMITTEE ON FOREIGN RELATIONS,
Washington, DC.

The subcommittee met, pursuant to notice, at 2:17 p.m., in room SD–419, Dirksen Senate Office Building, Hon. Christopher A. Coons, chairman of the subcommittee, presiding.

Present: Senators Coons, Cardin, Durbin, Udall, Lugar, and Isakson.

OPENING STATEMENT OF HON. CHRISTOPHER A. COONS, U.S. SENATOR FROM DELAWARE

Senator COONS. I am pleased to convene today's hearing of the African Affairs Subcommittee, and I am honored to be joined with my friend and partner, the ranking minority member of the subcommittee, Senator Isakson, and the ranking minority member of the full committee, Senator Lugar.

I thank them both for joining me today. I would also like to thank our distinguished witnesses, Ambassador David Shinn, adjunct professor at George Washington University and former U.S. Ambassador to both Ethiopia and Burkina Faso; Professor Deborah Brautigam, professor at American University and senior fellow at the International Food Policy Research Institute; and Mr. Stephen Hayes, president and CEO of the Corporate Council on Africa.

Today's hearing will take a hard look at China's rapidly expanding role on the African Continent and consider how it is affecting American interests. In my view, the United States isn't just ceding its potential economic leadership in Africa to China, it may be ceding its political and moral leadership there as well.

We will discuss today whether China's expanded reach should serve as a wakeup call for enhanced United States trade and investment, and we will take a close look at whether China's growing influence in Africa may counter or even possibly undermine United States development, diplomacy, and other values-driven goals in the region.

Finally, we will also consider areas of common interest between the United States and China in Africa that could provide the basis for enhanced bilateral and multilateral cooperation.

China's reach in Africa has grown dramatically in the past decade, and the rate of increased Chinese trade and investment in

Africa is truly staggering. Between 2000 and 2010, trade between China and African nations grew by more than 1,000 percent.

As you can see in our first chart here today, U.S. trade with Africa grew during this period as well, partly due to the passage of the Africa Growth and Opportunity Act, or AGOA. But the average rate of growth in China's trade with Africa outpaced that of the United States by 100 percent.

China clearly sees Africa for what it is, a continent of immense opportunity. Africa is home to 6 of the world's 10 fastest-growing economies over the past decade. Increased rates of return on foreign investment, vast natural resources, and a rapidly growing middle class have all made Africa an increasingly important player in the global economy.

But as the continent has grown economically, it has continued to also have significant development needs. The United States and China are both investing in that development, but doing so in very different ways. While we share some common interests in Africa that are at times complementary we should be clear-eyed about the very different nature of our engagement.

First, our structures of government spending are different. The United States clearly distinguishes between Government assistance and private investment, while the line between public and private sectors in China is often blurred and involves many state-owned enterprises.

The Chinese Government can offer financing and concessionary loans to African governments to build large infrastructure projects, in some cases with no interest required for up to 20 years and, at the same time, negotiate contracts with those same governments for mineral and oil extraction.

While the United States invests diplomatic capital in the promotion of democracy, freedom of expression, and human rights, our leverage on African officials and governments is significantly weakened when those regimes can simply turn to China for support with essentially no value strings attached.

If there is one message I wish to convey in this hearing, it is that the long-term American objective of promoting open societies in Africa—countries that embrace transparency and democracy, respect the environment, and protect human rights—is being challenged in some ways by China's approach to Africa. By offering an alternative source of investment and development, China offers African regimes economic opportunity at times at the expense of government reform and in a manner that may not directly benefit the average African.

This highlights a second key distinction. In my view, the U.S. Government has been investing in the people of Africa, while the Chinese Government has been investing in the infrastructure of Africa. It is tough to say precisely, given a real lack of transparency, but experts estimate roughly 70 percent of Chinese assistance to Africa comes in the form of financing for roads, stadiums, and government buildings, often built with Chinese materials and often by Chinese laborers.

China is rarely transferring significant technology to Africa, nor employing many Africans. In contrast, more than 70 percent, as this chart shows, of U.S. Government spending is directed toward investment in the African people, primarily through health programs to combat HIV/AIDS, malaria, tuberculosis, and other diseases. These programs build upon the strong legacy of U.S. investment in global health established by former Presidents Clinton and Bush.

America's extensive public sector investments in Africa are often not as visible as those of China. Many Africans can point proudly to Chinese-built roads, buildings, or hospitals in their capital without realizing that many of the doctors or nurses there have been trained by Americans, medical supplies were provided by the U.S. Government, and that many rural health clinics that are lowering maternal mortality rates, vaccinating children, and donating mosquito nets across Africa are, in fact, often United States funded. We may be, in sum, winning the war on disease while losing the battle for hearts and minds.

As we think about next steps for United States public and private sectors, we must gain, I believe, a better understanding of China's role and motives and take steps to ensure the United States is not missing out on critical opportunities in Africa.

Senator Durbin, who I am pleased has joined us here today, is proposing legislation to do just that. It aims to create jobs in America by increasing United States exports to Africa by at least 200 percent in the next 10 years. This is absolutely critical because China has outpaced the United States in growth of exports over the last decade by nearly 3-to-1, as shown by our last chart.

I want to thank Senator Durbin for initiating this legislation. I believe we need a comprehensive United States trade strategy for Africa, and we must work with existing resources—with the Ex-Im Bank, with OPIC, and USTR—to find ways to expand bilateral, regional, and multilateral trade opportunities. More United States companies selling their goods in Africa translates to more American jobs.

There are many tools by which we can and should take a more assertive approach to expanding the scope of United States investment in Africa, and in my view, the U.S. Government must pursue an assertive strategy that aims to capitalize on the vast array of opportunities in Africa. We cannot simply afford to lose out to China in the private sector, while in the public sector we must ensure our values are not undermined by an expansive political and economic agenda by China.

I look forward to hearing from our distinguished witnesses how the United States can achieve these objectives, but first, I would like to turn to Senator Isakson for his opening statement.

Senator Isakson.

OPENING STATEMENT OF HON. JOHNNY ISAKSON, U.S. SENATOR FROM GEORGIA

Senator ISAKSON. Well, thanks, Chairman Coons, for calling this hearing, particularly with regard to the role of China in Africa.

I had the pleasure of traveling with Senator Coons to West Africa earlier this year, where we went to Ghana, Benin, and Nigeria and saw firsthand the benefits of United States investment and the Millennium Challenge Compact in particular in Ghana, where we actually saw the execution of that compact.

They will be coming back for a second compact. And as President Mills told us in his office that the focus on lack of corruption, the focus on better governance, the focus on democracy, which was a quid pro quo for the Millennium Challenge investment, has, in fact, made Ghana a better country.

And I commend President Mills on his movement toward democracy. I hope Goodluck Jonathan in Nigeria, who is the first successfully democratically elected Nigerian President with somewhat minimal violence taking place, will follow the role of President Mills and President Yayi in Cotonou. Benin is also moving forward. Their port project, which is also an MCC compact, is in its final year, and it has been an excellent example of the MCC challenge investment in Africa.

But there is no question that the Chinese have a significant role in Africa, and I think the chairman has done a good job of outlining the role that they are taking, which is more in their own self-interest than in the interest of the African people.

And while their investment level may be higher in dollars, I think our investment level in the rights, the health, and the safety and security of the African people is greater. And it is my hope that over time that will win the hearts of the African Continent because I do think Africa is the continent of the 21st century for the United States of America.

They could be a great energy partner, a great consumer of our goods and services, and we could have a great partnership to grow and prosper together. Hopefully, what was started out in the Bush administration in terms of PEPFAR and MCC compacts will continue, and I certainly intend to support both of them, as I have in the past.

As well as I want to acknowledge what the chairman referred to obliquely, and that is the private sector investment by Americans compassionately in the continent of Africa. Malaria now doesn't exist on Zanzibar. And even though it is an island, it is a little easier to control, thanks to the Rotary Clubs International and the investment they are making in bed nets throughout that continent, it is amazing the effect we are having on that.

The same thing is true with measles and polio. The same thing is also true in many other areas. Kiwanis International has adopted as its No. 1 national project the eradication of tetanus in Africa, which is also critically important.

And the Coca-Cola Company—that is a hometown company of mine, so I will brag about the home front for a second—is investing $30 million a year in clean water projects. And Senator Coons and I drank clean water out of a Coca-Cola-provided treatment facility in a village that had never had clean water before.

And the great thing they are doing is they are charging them 7 cents a day for 5 gallons of water to teach them that it takes money to keep the plant running. They are going to turn the plant over for nothing to the African people, but they will pay for its continued maintenance and upkeep by their paying for the water they get every day.

So a lot of the basic principles of our competitive free enterprise system and the compassion of the American people are paying great benefits. But it should not go unnoted that some African leaders prefer no-strings-attached investment, and they like China for that reason.

There is no question that China is abusing some of its interests. And this week, Human Rights Watch will issue a report that alleges the Chinese routinely bribe or threaten miners to keep them from reporting accidents and problems in Zambian-operated mines, which is just one example of how they are looking the other way on the best interests of the human rights of those people.

I think, in the end, our investment in the health, safety, and welfare of folks is important and can win the hearts of the Africans over, but we cannot allow China to buy away that friendship from the United States.

Thank you, Mr. Chairman.

Senator COONS. Thank you, Senator Isakson.

Senator Lugar, did you want to make an opening statement?

Senator LUGAR. No.

Senator COONS. Senator Durbin.

OPENING STATEMENT OF HON. RICHARD J. DURBIN, U.S. SENATOR FROM ILLINOIS

Senator DURBIN. Thank you for this hearing.

And I want to thank the witnesses who are here, and many of them have worked with our office on this issue. And I think that we are finally identifying in the Foreign Relations Committee an issue which could have grave consequences in the future.

I believe Africa is an emerging continent with an emerging middle class and holds great economic significance in the 21st century. China obviously discovered that quite a few years ago. And the question now is what we will do as a nation to compete on the continent of Africa, and I know that there will be some discussion here about particulars.

And I thank you, Mr. Chairman, for bringing us together.

Senator COONS. Thank you.

We will now turn to our witnesses, starting with Ambassador Shinn, followed by Dr. Brautigam, and finally by Mr. Hayes.

I would appreciate it if you could condense your remarks to no more than 5 minutes. Your full testimony will be placed in the record where it will be available to other members of the committee, and in the record.

So, if you would, please, Ambassador Shinn.

STATEMENT OF HON. DAVID SHINN, ADJUNCT PROFESSOR, GEORGE WASHINGTON UNIVERSITY, WASHINGTON, DC

Ambassador SHINN. Thank you very much, Chairman Coons, for inviting me, and I also thank the committee.

China has essentially four hard interests in Africa. First is maintaining or increasing access to energy, minerals, timber, and agricultural products; second, developing good relations with all African countries so that China can count on their support in regional and international forums; third, increasing significantly China's exports to Africa; and last, ending Taiwan's official diplomatic presence in Africa and replacing it with recognition of Beijing.

The magnitude of China's involvement in Africa since the mid 1990s has grown exponentially. China has diplomatic relations with 50 of the 54 African countries today. Beijing has an Embassy in every one of those countries except one, Somalia.

China has particularly developed an effective state-to-state relationship with African leaders. Hu Jintao has made six trips to multiple African countries—two as Vice President, four as President.

Each year since 1991, China's Foreign Minister has made his first visit abroad anywhere in the world, usually in January, to an African country. China has a layer of high-level contact, the Communist Party of China, that frequently interacts with African officials. This is a layer, of course, the United States doesn't have a counterpart for.

China has no military bases in Africa but has some security interaction with all 50 countries on the continent with which it has diplomatic relations. China has passed the United States and has become Africa's most important trade partner since 2009. China imports about one-third of all of its oil imports from Africa. China also imports huge quantities of cobalt, manganese, tantalum, copper, iron ore, and other minerals.

There is a lot of confusion surrounding China's investment in Africa in terms of the numbers and in terms of the definition. Suffice it to say that it is probably somewhere in the vicinity of almost $40 billion. It is possible that today China is investing more in Africa than any other single country.

Large Chinese loans, often with concessionary terms, are grabbing a lot of the headlines about China-Africa interaction. In the case of Angola, China has signed about 14.5 billion dollars' worth of these concessionary loans. With Ghana, recently $13 billion. China has also stepped up its efforts on soft power in Africa.

Now what are the implications for the United States? I think the heightened engagement in Africa by China since the mid-1990s has very important implications for the United States.

Certainly, if you look at relationships with countries like Zimbabwe and Sudan, it provides a real option for China that did not previously exist. But even countries that have good relations with the United States find themselves in a position where they can be a lot more selective in terms of the advice that they accept from the United States because they might be able to obtain support from China.

On the commercial side, a company like Boeing continues to do well in Africa. It also has no Chinese competition. On the other hand, electronic giants like Hewlett-Packard, Motorola, Siemens, and Ericsson are increasingly losing business to Chinese companies such as Huawei and ZTE.

The easy financing offered by Chinese state banks, lower bids on projects by Chinese state-controlled construction companies, and the fact that these companies have a ubiquitous presence on the African Continent make it difficult for American and Western companies to compete.

China's growing interest in African raw materials should not pose a problem for the United States, except to the extent that Chinese demand pushes up global commodity prices.

China's growing use of soft power in Africa should prod the United States to do better. For the time being, China poses no security threat to the United States in Africa and probably will not do so for at least the next 5 years.

Other emerging powers are also playing a great role in Africa, and attention needs to be given to them. There has been the return of Russia. India is becoming a significant competitor of China on the continent. But Brazil, Iran, Turkey, Saudi Arabia, United Arab Emirates, Vietnam, Thailand, Indonesia, Malaysia, Singapore, and Cuba are all returning or engaging for the first time in a major way.

Areas for cooperation with China include the health sector, particularly, antimalarial programs, also neglected tropical diseases like hookworm and schistosomiasis; the agricultural sector; and U.N. peacekeeping operations.

In terms of coordinated diplomatic engagement, I think there are areas where the two countries can collaborate and in even controversial places like South Sudan and Sudan, where there today are some mutual interests. While the United States and China will continue to have important differences in their approach to Africa, it is in the interest of both governments to seek out those areas where they can cooperate.

I thank you very much for your time, Mr. Chairman.

[The prepared statement of Ambassador Shinn follows:]

PREPARED STATEMENT OF HON. DAVID H. SHINN

I thank Chairman Kerry of the Senate Foreign Relations Committee and Chairman Coons of the Subcommittee on African Affairs for inviting me to participate in this hearing. I have been researching China-Africa relations intensively over the past 5 years in connection with a book scheduled for publication next spring. Unless noted otherwise, the statistics and analysis contained in this testimony refer to all 54 countries in Africa. China tends not to make a distinction between sub-Saharan Africa and North Africa as the U.S. Government often does.

CHINA'S INTERESTS IN AFRICA

China generally does not discuss its "hard" interests in Africa. Rather, it emphasizes several general themes such as respect for African countries' sovereignty and development policies, support for African development, cooperation with Africa in the United Nations and multilateral forums, and learning from each other. China also urges African countries to accept the "one China" principle by recognizing Beijing.

Based on my analysis, China has four "hard" interests in Africa:
- Maintaining or increasing access to energy, minerals, timber, and agricultural products.
- Developing good relations with all African countries so that China can count on their support in regional and international forums.
- Increasing significantly China's exports to Africa, especially as the economies of African states become more robust and Africans increase their disposable income.
- Ending Taiwan's official diplomatic presence in Africa and replacing it with recognition of Beijing.

I should point out that you can substitute the United States for China in each of the first three interests; they apply as much to the United States as they do to China. I would argue that the United States has several additional interests that do not yet apply in a meaningful way to China. First, the United States has an interest in military aircraft over flight and landing in African countries and access to their ports by U.S. naval vessels. Second, the United States puts a high priority on countering a series of issues—terrorism, piracy, drug trafficking, money laundering, etc.—that pose a threat to American interests. While these issues may eventually become important Chinese interests, they have not yet reached that level.

CURRENT DIMENSIONS OF CHINESE ENGAGEMENT IN AFRICA

While China is not new to Africa, the magnitude of its engagement with the continent has grown exponentially since the mid-1990s. This period has coincided with enormous industrial growth in China, the need to import increasing quantities of raw materials to support China's manufacturing sector, and China's ability to export significantly more competitively priced products to Africa. China's interest in access to raw materials reinforced its longstanding policy of developing strong political relations with as many countries as possible in Africa.

China has diplomatic relations with 50 of the 54 African countries. Four—Burkina Faso, Swaziland, Gambia, and São Tomé and Principe—recognize Taipei. Beijing has an embassy in all but one of the 50 countries. The exception is Somalia where the security situation in Mogadishu precludes a physical presence. All 50 African countries that recognize China except the Comoro Islands and recently independent South Sudan have embassies in Beijing. Although the United States has diplomatic relations with all 54 African countries, it too has embassies in only 50. It closed embassies in the Seychelles and Comoro Islands to save money and never opened in São Tomé and Principe. Like China, it is not in Somalia for security reasons. China has more consulates in Africa than does the United States.

China is especially effective at state-to-state relations and attaches particular importance to high-level personal contact. Hu Jintao has made six trips to multiple African countries—two as Vice President and four as President. China's Premier is a frequent visitor to Africa. Each year since 1991, China's Foreign Minister has made his first visit abroad, usually in January, to an African country. China has a layer of high-level contact—senior Communist Party of China officials—that frequently visits Africa to expand relations with African party and executive branch officials. The United States has no similar counterpart nor does it rely as heavily on Presidential and Vice Presidential visits to Africa. If you exclude annual visits to the United Nations' headquarters in New York by African leaders, where some do have meetings with the American President, Chinese leaders extend more invitations to African leaders to visit China than the United States extends to visit Washington. The Communist Party of China frequently invites leaders of African political parties to visit China.

China has no military bases in Africa but has some security interaction, however modest, with all 50 countries that recognize Beijing. China's share of the conventional arms market in sub-Saharan Africa is about 15 percent. The percentage is higher for small arms and light weapons. High-level military visits are an important part of the security relationship. Twenty-eight African countries have defense attachés in Beijing while 16 Chinese defense attaché offices in Africa are accredited to some 30 African countries. China has about 1,600 military/police personnel serving in six of the United Nation's peacekeeping operations in Africa. Most of the personnel are in Darfur, South Sudan, Liberia, and the Democratic Republic of the Congo. It has small numbers in Côte d'Ivoire and the Western Sahara. Since 2008, China has positioned two frigates and a tender in the Gulf of Aden to combat Somali piracy. Following a lapse in naval visits to African ports since 2002, this engagement in the Gulf of Aden has led to a recent increase in Chinese visits to African ports.

By contrast, the United States has a designated military command—AFRICOM—for Africa located in Germany, a base with about 3,000 military and civilian personnel in Djibouti for countering terrorism, a new facility in Ethiopia for operating drones and significantly more defense attaché offices than does China. While the United States pays a higher proportion of U.N. peacekeeping costs in Africa than does China, it has less than 30 personnel assigned to the six operations in Africa. The United States has played a leading role in the antipiracy operation in the Gulf of Aden and western Indian Ocean. U.S. military ships and airplanes regularly visit African cities and ports. The United States also engages in far more training of African military forces than does China.

China passed the United States and became Africa's most important trade partner in 2009. It continues to hold that position. China-Africa trade (exports and imports) totaled $127 billion in 2010 compared to $113 billion for United States-Africa trade. While China's trade with Africa has been growing at a rapid pace since the turn of the century, it constitutes only about 4 percent of China's global trade. China's trade is, however, proportionally more important for Africa and makes up about 13 percent of the continent's total trade. Except for 2009, when Africa collectively had a large trade deficit with China, its trade has been roughly in balance. This is in sharp contrast with U.S.-Africa trade, which has witnessed a large U.S. trade deficit over the past decade, primarily due to large oil imports from Africa. In 2010, the United States imported 85 billion dollars' worth of goods from Africa and exported $28 billion to Africa. There are huge differences in China's trade balance with individual African countries. Some 11 African oil and mineral exporters have major surpluses with China, while the remainder, which includes the poorer countries, has significant trade deficits with China or the trade is roughly in balance.

China imports about one-third of its total oil imports from Africa. Of China's 10 most important trading partners in Africa, 6 (Angola, Sudan, Nigeria, Algeria, Libya, and the Republic of Congo) export large quantities of oil to China. In 2009, oil and gas accounted for 64 percent of all African exports to China. While that constitutes a lot of oil, it is only about 13 percent of total African oil exports. The United States and EEC countries each import almost one-third of Africa's total oil exports, significantly more than China imports. On the other hand, the United States imports relatively modest quantities of African mineral products while China imports huge quantities of cobalt, manganese, tantalum, copper, iron ore, and other minerals. In 2009, iron ore and metals accounted for 24 percent of all African exports to China. It also imports timber and may look increasingly to Africa for agricultural products. Without these raw materials from Africa and other parts of the world, China would be unable to sustain its manufacturing capacity and maintain its high GDP growth rate. A sharp decrease in China's economic growth would be a direct threat to the current leadership of the Communist Party of China. Access to African raw materials is a long-term strategic interest.

While China continues to increase significantly its imports from Africa, it is also increasing its total exports and the value added component to Africa. In 2000, China's exports to Africa consisted largely of textiles and clothing (28 percent), machinery and transportation equipment (27 percent), and other manufactured goods (26 percent). By 2009, Chinese exports to Africa shifted to high-end capital goods, especially communications equipment (20 percent), road transport vehicles (19 percent), and electronic machinery (18 percent).

China's State Council issued a white paper in December 2010 that stated China's direct investment in Africa reached $9.33 billion by the end of 2009. There is considerable confusion surrounding this figure and on China's definition of direct investment. For reasons that are not clear, I believe most official Chinese figures for investment totals in Africa significantly understate the real amount. Even Chinese sources cannot agree on the amount of FDI that has gone into Africa. The official Xinhua News Agency reported last month that by the end of 2010, China had invested about $40 billion in more than 2,000 enterprises in 50 African countries. This figure included investments of $2.1 billion in 2010 alone. While the correct total FDI figure is probably much closer to $40 billion than to $9.33 billion, Western countries collectively have invested much more in Africa, primarily because they started earlier. By the end of 2008, for example, the United States had invested a cumulative total of $37 billion in sub-Saharan Africa alone.

It is possible that today China is investing more in Africa than any other single country. The primary recipients of Chinese FDI have been South Africa, Nigeria, Zambia, Sudan, Algeria, and Egypt, all major oil or mineral exporters except for Egypt. Interestingly, the State Council's December 2010 white paper reported that by the end of 2009, African countries had invested $9.93 billion in China; i.e., more than the paper reported China had invested in Africa! It is difficult to document where this much African money has been invested.

One of the other persons testifying today is far more knowledgeable than I on China's aid to Africa. I will describe this component of China's engagement.

The headline grabbing stories of Chinese engagement in Africa rarely involve investment or aid. More often, they concern large Chinese loans, often with concessionary financing, used by African countries to finance infrastructure projects. In recent years, China has signed loan agreements, for example, with Angola for about $14.5 billion, Ghana for $13 billion, and the Democratic Republic of the Congo for $6.5 billion. Most of this money will be used to finance roads, dams, refineries, buildings, railways, etc., by Chinese construction companies and be repaid in oil or minerals. China has become the major builder in Africa.

China has also stepped up its soft power efforts in Africa. The Xinhua news service has more than 20 bureaus in Africa and regional offices in Cairo and Nairobi. Xinhua competes directly with Reuters, AP, and Bloomberg for reporting on events in Africa. There are at last 22 Confucius Institutes in Africa that focus on teaching Chinese language, culture, and history and the number continues to grow. China is increasing its radio transmission to Africa in various languages, has a transmitting facility in Kenya, and has rebroadcast arrangements with countries around the continent. It trains a variety of Africans, including diplomats and journalists, and in 2009 increased to 4,000 the number of full scholarships it offers to African students each year.

IMPLICATIONS FOR U.S. POLICY AND INTERESTS

This heightened engagement in Africa by China since the mid-1990s has important implications for the United States. China now offers African countries another political and especially economic alternative to the United States and the West generally. Countries such as Zimbabwe and Sudan, which have poor relations with the United States and the West, have taken maximum advantage of this situation. China does not engage in conditionality, except for the "one China" principle and tying its aid and loans to Chinese companies and materials. As a result, China (and a number of other countries) ignores Western sanctions against Zimbabwe and Sudan and continues to be one of the most important suppliers of military equipment to both countries. As a major supplier of small arms and light weapons across the continent, Chinese weapons are increasingly showing up in conflict zones. There is no evidence China is selling weapons to rebel groups, but as more weapons appear in Africa, the greater is the chance they find their way into conflicts. In fairness, weapons from all major arms manufacturing countries, including the United States, are making their way into these conflicts.

Even countries that have good relations with the United States, such as Ethiopia, Kenya, Angola, Ghana, and South Africa, find themselves in a position where they can be much more selective in taking advice from the United States. African states under pressure from the United States and the West to improve their human rights and governance practices are less likely to do so when they know they can rely on China for support. China holds a veto power in the U.N. Security Council and Africa has three nonpermanent seats on the Council. Africa is well represented in organizations of interest to China such as the U.N. Human Rights Council and the World Trade Organization. China makes every effort to cultivate the maximum number of African countries on all issues of interest to Beijing that arise in international forums. In some cases, like-minded African governments use the Chinese just as the Chinese use them, for example when contentious issues affecting China or a particular African nation arise in the Human Rights Council. When Tibet became an issue in 2008, China leaned on the Africans to remain silent or even make supportive statements. They did. African countries can depend on China to avoid raising controversial African human rights issues in the U.N. Human Rights Council and perhaps even to support them when they are criticized by Western countries.

China does not have a good record in Africa for worker safety and labor practices. It also receives criticism for allowing harmful and counterfeit products manufactured by private Chinese companies into African countries. The same is true for engaging in corruption although there are a few indications that China is beginning to see corruption as a negative factor for doing business in Africa. The United States generally has a good record in these areas and would prefer to see improvements in Africa. Sensitive to all of these criticisms, China is seeking ways to deal with these problems but is slow to find solutions. China's relations with strong, independent African labor unions are not cordial and labor standards in China are sometimes less stringent than in some African countries. African nations do not have the institutions to keep harmful and counterfeit products from entering and China has either not figured out or is not interested in preventing these problems at the source.

The United States and the West had a major headstart over China on investment and commercial engagement with Africa. This is especially true in the energy and mineral sector where so much Western investment has gone over the years. As a result, there has not yet been much head-to-head competition except in the case of winning large commercial contracts where China is pulling ahead in many sectors. A company like Boeing continues to do well in Africa and has no Chinese competition. On the other hand, electronic giants such as Hewlett-Packard, Motorola, Siemens, and Ericsson are increasingly losing business to Chinese companies such as Huawei and ZTE. The Chinese companies offer much lower prices for products that many Africans believe are of adequate, if somewhat lower, quality compared to their Western alternatives. In addition, Huawei and ZTE are creating large sales and marketing offices in Africa.

The easy financing offered by Chinese state banks, lower bids on projects by Chinese state-controlled construction companies and the fact that the companies now have a ubiquitous presence on the ground throughout much of Africa, make it difficult for American and Western companies to compete. Private Western companies generally function independently of their governments and often find it hard to compete with the package proposals presented by the Chinese Government and their state-owned or controlled companies. This is, however, a structural issue that the United States and the West will have to work around or simply become more competitive.

China's growing interest in African raw materials should not pose a problem for the United States except to the extent that Chinese demand pushes up global commodity prices. This could lead to higher prices paid by the United States and the rest of the world. So long as American companies and consumers have the money to pay for the product, African countries will continue to sell to the U.S. market. The problem is on the U.S. export side. It is not competing well against China in Africa. This is a problem that American companies will have to solve, although agencies like the Export-Import Bank can help. In some cases, American companies just have to take more interest in African markets and accept more risk.

China's growing use of soft power in Africa should prod the United States to respond. Security concerns and fortress embassies in many African countries make outreach difficult. Numerous American libraries have been shut down. The Voice of America and government-sponsored programs for sending future African leaders to the United States are under budgetary pressure. All of these trends are in the wrong direction. This is the time to reach out on all fronts and be more accessible to African publics. These programs are not expensive and they have the potential to achieve an enormous amount of good will.

For the time being, China poses no security threat to the United States in Africa and probably will not do so over the next 5 years or so. China is, however, expanding its naval capacity. This year it held sea trials for its first aircraft carrier. It has significantly expanded its submarine fleet and clearly intends to build a carrier force. One reason for building this capacity is to make China less reliant on the U.S. Navy for protection of Chinese vessels in the Indian Ocean. Some 80 percent of China's imported oil comes from Africa and the Middle East and passes through the Strait of Malacca. Once China has a major naval presence in the Indian Ocean, it will bump up against the U.S. Navy and, more importantly, the Indian Navy.

OTHER EMERGING POWERS IN AFRICA

China is only one, albeit the most important, of the emerging powers to assert itself in Africa. The European countries, Japan, South Korea, Canada, and Australia continue their longstanding engagement in Africa, but together with the United States have been somewhat more reserved since the end of the cold war. Russia has recently returned to Africa in a major way following its retreat from the continent after the breakup of the Soviet Union. China and other emerging powers have been the big story in Africa over the past decade.

Only India approaches the ability of China to compete in Africa and it is probably a decade behind China. China's trade with Africa is 2½ times that of India. China has almost twice as many embassies in Africa as India. Its investment and aid are much higher. On the other hand, India is physically closer, has a language advantage, and has stronger cultural links. India also has 7,000 U.N. military and police peacekeepers in Africa compared to China's 1,600. India's naval presence in the western Indian Ocean is much stronger than China's and India has been developing security agreements with countries in the Indian Ocean and along the East African coast.

Although well behind China and India, Brazil has made its presence felt throughout much of Africa, not just the Lusophone countries. Iran has focused its attention on northeastern Africa but is expanding its relations throughout the continent in an effort to escape isolation. Turkey stepped up its engagement in Africa beginning in 2005 and is an important player in North Africa and the Horn of Africa. Its engagement is heavily business-based but also has a strong cultural, religious, and educational component. Other emerging countries that are either reengaging in Africa or arriving for the first time include Saudi Arabia, United Arab Emirates, Vietnam, Thailand, Indonesia, Malaysia, Singapore, and Cuba.

This situation is resulting in a much more crowded diplomatic playing field. While it provides more opportunities for African countries to obtain aid, investment, and trade, it complicates American diplomacy. It argues for greater understanding about the meaning of these developments and, in some cases, a reassessment of U.S. policies toward Africa and the coalitions needed for diplomatic successes.

AREAS FOR COOPERATION WITH CHINA

There are several inherent challenges for U.S.-China cooperation in Africa. It is necessary to overcome longstanding suspicions between the two countries, fostered in part by different philosophies toward governance. Perhaps more important, it is necessary to convince the African countries that the United States and China are not trying to gang up on them. There is a tendency in many African countries to want to play China off against the United States in order to obtain an advantage.

They often fail to distinguish that there are areas where China and the United States can cooperate and, at the same time, benefit the African country in question.

If these two concerns can be overcome, and they have been in several cases, there are areas when China and the United States can work together for the mutual benefit of African countries. This occurred in Liberia, for example, where China and the United States collaborated in construction of the military barracks at Bonga for a U.N. peacekeeping operation and the two countries agreed to join forces to combat malaria. Successful cooperation depends heavily on the active engagement of the American and Chinese Ambassadors and key Embassy staff on the ground. If they do not support the proposed collaboration, it probably will not happen. At the same time, there must be signals from Washington and Beijing that both governments are fully behind the cooperative endeavor.

The United States and China have particular strengths in the health sector that can collaboratively improve the situation in Africa. This is especially true in anti-malarial programs where China is constructing 30 malaria treatment centers in Africa and providing antimalarial drugs such as artemisinin. USAID supports a holistic program that includes insecticide-treated bed nets and the President's Malaria Initiative has a goal of reducing mortality by half in target countries. Other areas for cooperation are neglected tropical diseases, especially hookworm and schistosomiasis, where each country has important expertise to reduce the threat. Improvement in nutrition and pandemic preparedness are other possible problems for collaboration. Both China and the United States have considerable experience with African agriculture, another area where they could combine their experience and lessons learned.

While the United States and China want to export more to Africa, they could also work to build the export capacity of African countries by building their competitiveness in global markets. Both countries could provide technical assistance for this purpose. China has shown a growing interest in improved corporate social responsibility in China and in the context of Chinese companies operating in Africa. This is also a priority goal for the United States and one where American companies have considerable experience. Both countries have demonstrated their concern in recent years over the negative impact of climate change and environmental degradation. African countries are deeply concerned about climate change's impact on the continent and might welcome a joint approach from China and the United States.

The United States provides the single largest amount of funding for U.N. and African Union peacekeeping operations. Washington welcomes the assignment of Chinese soldiers, mostly engineering, transportation, and medical personnel, to U.N. peacekeeping operations in Africa. U.S. and China's interests generally overlap when it comes to African peacekeeping operations; specific projects for collaboration should be identified. Similarly, the two countries generally have common interests in helping African coastal states to reduce piracy, smuggling, illegal fishing, drug trafficking, and threats to offshore oil facilities. Although Chinese ships operate independently in the Gulf of Aden antipiracy operation, the United States Navy and China's Navy have a good working relationship. The U.S. Coast Guard has been particularly successful in cooperating with Chinese counterpart organizations. There may be an opportunity for extending this cooperation to Africa. Countering drug smuggling across Africa and improving disaster relief are additional areas that lend themselves to U.S.-China cooperation for the mutual benefit of Africans.

COORDINATED DIPLOMATIC ENGAGEMENT IN AFRICA

There are a number of conflicts and crises where the interests of the United States and China are similar. Both countries usually seek stability in Africa. China normally supports whatever government is in power irrespective of its pedigree or ideology. While China is quick to shift its allegiance to a new regime as occurred in recent years in Niger and Guinea, it does not want to be seen as behind regime change. As a result, China has no inclination to encourage governmental change in places such as Harare or Khartoum. If it suspects the United States is seeking regime change in any particular country, China will keep its distance. Coordinated diplomatic engagement also tends to raise suspicions among some African parties that the United States and China are ganging up against them. China is especially sensitive to this charge and will be reluctant to work with the United States on any issue where this is the perception by one or more of the African parties involved in the conflict.

On the other hand, here has been little difference in the U.S. and China's policies toward Somalia. Both countries support the Transitional Federal Government and want to counter terrorism, although China is probably not prepared to accept some of Washington's tactics. Nevertheless, Somalia is a conflict that lends itself to continuing quiet collaboration. The United States encouraged China to play a more active role in resolving the conflict in Darfur. Eventually it did but only after some difficult episodes in U.S.-China interaction. Today, China has an interest in maintaining close ties to the Bashir government in Khartoum and the new government in South Sudan. It owns much of the oil infrastructure in the Republic of Sudan while 75 percent of the oil now originates in South Sudan. China has been surprisingly successful in building a good relationship with Salva Kiir's government in Juba. There may well be ways for China and the United States to coordinate diplomacy as they help to resolve the enormous challenges facing both countries. China will consider such collaboration, however, only if it is convinced that the United States is not seeking regime change in Khartoum.

Other troubled parts of Africa where there are no obvious differences in U.S. or China's policy include Côte d'Ivoire, Madagascar, and Guinea. They are candidates for coordinated diplomatic engagement. More complicated conflicts that might lend themselves to coordinated diplomatic engagement include the Democratic Republic of the Congo and Libya. China has or is developing significant interests in both countries and may be reluctant to team up with the United States and other Western countries, but it is worth exploring.

While the United States and China will continue to have important differences in their approach to Africa, it is in the interest of both governments to seek out those areas where they can cooperate.

Senator COONS. Thank you, Ambassador Shinn.
Dr. Brautigam.

STATEMENT OF DEBORAH BRAUTIGAM, PH.D., PROFESSOR, AMERICAN UNIVERSITY AND SENIOR RESEARCH FELLOW, INTERNATIONAL FOOD POLICY RESEARCH INSTITUTE, WASHINGTON, DC

Dr. BRAUTIGAM. Thank you very much for this opportunity to speak with you today. I appreciate it very much, and I am going to start by telling you a story.

Once upon a time, there was a very large, poor, resource-rich country, just emerging from a period of intense conflict. And that country decided to focus on development. "We need to modernize our infrastructure," they said. "We need to develop our ports." And soon, they had a visit from a wealthy Asian country that had already become a major consumer of their oil.

And that country said to them, "We will make you a bargain. We will give you a line of credit worth $10 billion, and you can use that credit to develop your ports. Our companies can help you develop your power plants and modernize your mines. And you can repay us with your oil."

Now, many in this poor country were very suspicious of this Asian power. But nonetheless, they agreed to this bargain, and the work began. Now, as you are listening to this story, you are probably thinking which two countries—China and Angola, China-Sudan, China and the DRC?

Well, actually, China was one of these countries. It was the large, poor country with oil. And the line of credit to be repaid with oil was offered by Japan in the late 1970s.

Now why am I telling you this story today? I am telling you this story for several different reasons. One is this arrangement was not based on aid. It was a market-rate line of credit that Japan offered to China. And the second is that China saw this as something that could be used for its benefit, for its development.

This was something that benefited Japan. They could sell goods and services to China, and it also benefited China because they could finance imports even though they didn't have an international credit rating.

Now China is operating in Africa using the frameworks that it has learned by being an Asian power, and some of those come from its relationship with Japan. And it is a very different model of engagement. And much of this does not actually involve official development aid. It is much closer to Japan's pattern of engagement in Asian countries.

So what does this involve? There are a lot of different tools and instruments that the Chinese have to engage in Africa that we don't have or that we have at a much smaller level. So, for example, they have resource-backed infrastructure loans.

I would argue that these are not concessional loans because the very large ones are all based on London Interbank Offered Rate. They are LIBOR plus margin-rate loans. These allow countries with poor credit ratings to borrow today and pay with tomorrow's exports.

They are setting up overseas economic zones that are attracting Chinese companies to come and set up manufacturing in Africa as costs become expensive in China. They have a $5 billion equity fund to encourage Chinese investment and joint ventures in Africa, and they have a $1 billion fund for small and medium enterprises. They are setting up agricultural demonstration centers that are trying to get Chinese agribusinesses involved in Africa.

So most of these are not about official aid, but they are about development. And more importantly, they are responding to the request by African leaders over and over again with assistance for help in building infrastructure and creating jobs in Africa.

Let me give you two quick stories. In Liberia, when Liberia emerged from war, Ellen Johnson Sirleaf said her main priority was roads and infrastructure. But the international donors were not providing roads and infrastructure. Then the Chinese stepped up and said, "We will build roads." And suddenly, the other donors became interested in roads.

When we look at what the Millennium Challenge Account is funding in Africa for African governments that are doing well and want to make their own decisions about how to spend their money, they are investing in infrastructure. So this is an important sector for Africans.

Now, China is not a new actor in Africa. Their presence is growing, as Ambassador Shinn has told us. Many of the things they are doing in Africa are nontransparent. We do not have information about them. That is a legacy of many things, partly because it is mainly business. We don't know a lot about how our own companies operate in Africa, even though we do have better data on that.

But the figures—I can talk about more in the question-and-answer period about what we know about the actual dimensions of engagement. But I want to make three final points. One is about realism versus alarmism.

China's rise in Africa should be seen in context. China is still a developing country. It has the norms and standards of a developing country and has much more in common with other developing countries than it has with us.

That means that it presents a lot of challenges. India, Brazil, and the other countries that Ambassador Shinn has just mentioned present the same kinds of challenges. They have the same levels of corruption. They operate in very similar kinds of ways. So this is a broader challenge, and it shouldn't be seen out of context.

The second is that we need much better information to make good policy. Our information about China in Africa is not good, and we are not doing a very good job of collecting better information.

And finally, we need to engage China multilaterally. We have a problem in that the arena for engagement that sets the rules and norms for how to engage internationally is the OECD, and China is not a member. We have to figure out a way to deal with this.

Thank you.

[The prepared statement of Dr. Brautigam follows:]

PREPARED STATEMENT DR. DEBORAH BRAUTIGAM[1]

China is not a new actor in Africa. Yet over the past decade, China's presence in Africa has grown remarkably, a reflection of China's rapid transformation as a global actor. This presents opportunities and challenges for Africa and its traditional development partners, including the United States. China's motives in Africa are twofold: diplomacy and business. There are more countries in Africa than in any other continent. Each has a vote in the United Nations, and many are also members of the World Trade Organization. Warm diplomatic ties are important for Chinese foreign policy goals, including competition with Taiwan, the effort to obtain market economy status at the United Nations, and Chinese efforts to emphasize sovereignty as a core foreign policy principle. On the other hand, Africa is an important source of raw materials and business opportunities for China's companies as they become global corporations.

CURRENT DIMENSIONS OF CHINESE ENGAGEMENT IN AFRICA

Current dimensions of Chinese engagement in Africa include trade, foreign direct investment, engineering contracts, development finance, development and humanitarian assistance, and military cooperation. I will focus here on the economic aspects. China's total trade with Africa in 2010 was $120.9 billion, about 4 percent of China's total trade with the world ($2972.7 billion). Chinese official figures for FDI in Africa 2007–2010 show an average of about $1.5 billion per year if one discounts the exceptional year 2008 when Industrial and Commercial Bank of China purchased 20 percent of South Africa's Standard Bank for around $5 billion. FDI in 2010 was reported to be $2.1 billion, with a stock of FDI at $13 billion.

Engineering contracts are enormous. In 2008, Chinese companies had nearly 3000 engineering contracts in Africa, valued at close to $40 billion (in 2008, Chinese companies had 180 separate engineering contracts in Libya, for example, valued at $10 billion, while earlier this year, the total in Libya had risen to $18 billion).[2] Some 187,396 Chinese were officially working in Africa in 2009, most on the large engineering contracts in Algeria, Libya, and Angola. Although there are exceptions, such as Angola, most of China's engineering business in Africa is not financed by the Chinese, but by African governments, development banks, bilateral banks, and private companies contracting with Chinese firms.

Some believe that the China is a bigger donor than the United States or the World Bank. This is far from the case. The United States disbursed a total of $29.7 billion (gross) in official development assistance in 2009, with $8 billion going to Africa, about 27 percent.[3] In 2010, the United States again budgeted $8 billion in aid for sub-Saharan Africa; global health and child survival came to $4.7 billion (57 percent).[4] The top five recipients of U.S. bilateral health assistance in sub-Saharan Africa in fiscal year 2012 were projected to be Kenya ($545 million), South Africa ($510 million), Nigeria ($471 million), Tanzania ($346 million), and Uganda ($323 million).[5] In the equivalent categories, China probably disbursed aid of about $3.1 billion (gross), with Africa receiving 45.7 percent, about $1.4 billion.[6] In 2010 alone, according to its annual report, the World Bank committed US$14.5 billion to 66 countries in IDA grants and soft loans, with cumulative commitments of US$222 billion since 1960. These differences are also reflected in staffing levels. USAID has a global staff of more than 8,000, of which almost 5,000 are host-country nationals; overseas projects employ considerable local personnel.[7] MOFCOM's Department of

Foreign Aid has about 100 staff, and the Export-Import Bank of China's Concessional Loan Department has another 100. The economic sections of Chinese embassies will also assign one or two people to manage the aid program locally (no host-country nationals appear to be employed).

In April 2011 the Chinese provided some of the first official figures on China's aid program: cumulative commitments of close to US$38 billion since the early 1950s and the end of 2009, broken down as follows (for all regions): [8]

- MOFCOM: cumulative US$16 bn in grants (not including debt relief), and US$11 bn in interest-free loans, some of which have been cancelled;
- China Eximbank: cumulative US$11 bn in concessional foreign aid loans

Africa has traditionally received between 40 and 50 percent of China's total aid annually. My estimates of Chinese aid disbursements suggest that on an annual basis, (Figure 1) China disbursed about US$1.3 billion in 2008, making it a mid-sized donor in Africa. (Chinese aid to Africa is growing rapidly; annual commitments could be more than 30 percent higher than disbursements.)

Figure 1: Major Donors, ODA to Africa, 2008
Disbursements, US$ bil

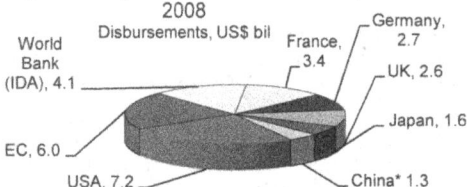

World Bank (IDA), 4.1 — France, 3.4 — Germany, 2.7 — UK, 2.6 — Japan, 1.6 — EC, 6.0 — USA, 7.2 — China* 1.3

Source: Brautigam, The Dragon's Gift, 2011 (2009).

In figuring out how to react to the rise of China in Africa, the United States first needs to understand how Chinese engagement works. For too long we have been trying to force the square pegs of Chinese engagement into the round holes of familiar Western patterns. Because we think of official development assistance (ODA) as the main currency for relations between Africa and the more developed world, we think this is what China is doing, instead of seeing their aid as a relatively small part of a far broader and more strategic engagement.

One of the major misconceptions of Chinese engagement in Africa is that it is largely financed by "concessional" loans, implying that it is a type of ODA (official development assistance). A 2010 background paper written for the OECD, for example, used the adjective "concessional" at least 27 times while writing in often general terms about the Chinese financing model in Africa.[9] Yet loose terminology like this is unhelpful for our understanding of how China operates overseas.

Most Chinese finance in Africa is not concessional. Indeed, Chinese banks reserve the term "concessional loan" only for the foreign aid loans issued by China Eximbank, with, as noted, a cumulative total of US$11 billion committed between 1995 and 2009. The term "concessional financing" should be reserved for "loans made by a government at an interest rate below the market rate as an indirect method of providing a subsidy."[10]

How much finance has China provided through other, nonconcessional instruments? The figures here are very approximate:

China Development Bank. In September 2010, China Development Bank said that it had made commitments of over US$10 billion to projects in Africa, and already disbursed US$5.6 billion to 35 projects in more than 30 African countries (People's Daily, 2010). This can be compared with an earlier announcement in March 2007, when CDB reported that it had financed 30 projects in Africa, for a total of about US$1 billion (Xinhua 2007).

China Eximbank. At the end of 2010, China Eximbank's outstanding loans in support of China's "Going Global" program totaled some US$41 bn worldwide.[11] In the year 2010, China Eximbank disbursed about US$7.6 bn in export sellers' credits for Chinese overseas investment and about US$1.3 bn to finance construction projects being implemented by Chinese firms. It is not clear how much of this was directed to Africa. China Eximbank president Li Ruogu said that his bank had committed over US$13 bn to Africa as of June 2007, and planned to extend up to US$20 bn in loans to Africa over the next 3 years.[12]

GOING OUT: INSTITUTIONS AND INSTRUMENTS IN CHINA'S
OVERSEAS DEVELOPMENT FINANCE

China's long history in Africa stretches over the Maoist period, (1949–1976), and the reform period, (1978-present). In the early 1980s, Chinese leaders reevaluated their aid program in view of its poor results, their limited funds and the need to focus more on their own development.[13] They announced to their African partners that China would need to "do more with less," focusing more on "mutually beneficial" cooperation rather than "one-way" aid.

At home, economist Chen Yun advised China to move toward the market cautiously, experimentally: "feeling for stones while crossing the stream." For the next decade, the Chinese experimented with ways to combine aid, trade, and investment in Africa. By the mid-1990s, the instruments were largely in place, although new experiments continue to be launched.

One of the changes was institutional. From the 1960s until 1995, Beijing financed its projects in Africa solely through an evolving set of departments and ministries that all focused on foreign economic cooperation (including aid) and trade. In 1994, as China continued to reform its economy in a market direction, Beijing established three policy banks.[14] Today, in the state-directed finance model that is common in East Asia's "developmental states" (Japan, Korea, Taiwan), China's Ministry of Commerce directly controls most of the instruments that provide actual government subsidies abroad.

Ministry of Commerce (MOFCOM). China's traditional aid instruments, zero-interest loans and grants, are financed directly out of China's budget for external assistance and are overseen by MOFCOM's Department of Aid to Foreign Countries, in cooperation with the respective regional departments of the Ministry of Foreign Affairs.

MOFCOM also has a variety of other funds, including the Special Fund for Foreign Economic and Technical Cooperation that can be used to support Chinese businesses, as long as they are carrying out the needs of China's economic diplomacy. One fund, for example, is used to support Chinese companies building six overseas special trade and economic cooperation zones in Africa.[15] These funds can be used for the partial reimbursement of preinvestment costs (feasibility studies, documents and consulting services, etc.) and some interest rate subsidies for bank loans.[16] They are not financed out of the external assistance budget.

China's Policy Banks. Two of China's policy banks (China Development Bank and China Eximbank) also operate overseas. Loans from policy banks are, as a Chinese analyst put it "heavily influenced by government policies and are not to operate in full compliance with market rules."[17] This does not mean that CDB and China Eximbank are allowed to be unprofitable or that they are directly subsidized by the government. Rather, as a recent study of CDB explains, with the Chinese Government standing behind them, policy banks have the same credit-rating as the Chinese Government, can raise funds by issuing bonds with that rating, and can take a longer term view with their loan investments.[18]

In 1995, China Eximbank was given sole responsibility for a new foreign aid instrument—concessional loans (you hui dai kuan). These are provided with a fixed interest rate, usually 2 or 3 percent, a grace period of 5 years, and a long repayment term (20 years). China's budget for foreign assistance subsidized the difference between the Eximbank's costs and the fixed interest rate. This allowed the Chinese Government to dramatically expand its resources for development assistance, but it also required more careful use of these resources, as the new loans were to be more carefully appraised for their financial feasibility. The Eximbank fully intended to be repaid. As the Eximbank's chief economist told an audience at a World Bank retreat: "it's the new lenders' problem if countries can't repay, not the Paris Club. We know we need a good, strong balance sheet." Although some Eximbank concessional loans have been rescheduled, there are no reports of any being canceled.

The majority of China Eximbank's lending instruments do not qualify as foreign aid. In 1998, they began offering export sellers credits (usually short to medium term) to Chinese firms to boost their ability to invest overseas and finance construction contracts.[19] In 2000, the bank launched export buyer's credits, rolling them out in Africa in 2005. These are usually issued in dollars, at London Interbank Offered Rate (LIBOR) or the Commercial Interest Rate of Reference (CIRR) rates prevailing in global markets. Preferential export buyer's credits (you hui mai fan xin dai) also exist. These are very similar to concessional loans, but are subsidized from a different budget.

Commercial Banks. In the past decade, several Chinese commercial banks—China Construction Bank, Industrial and Commercial Bank of China (ICBC), and Bank of China—have also set up offices in Africa to support Chinese companies' business.

One, ICBC, purchased 20 percent of South Africa's Standard Bank for around US$5 billion, and has since embarked on a number of joint projects across the continent.

China Africa Development Fund. The China Africa Development Fund (CAD Fund), overseen by CDB, provides equity capital. CDB provided the initial US$1 billion investment, and the CAD Fund was expected to raise finance for successive phases from other investors, with the goal of reaching US$5 billion. The fund's managers have stressed that this equity finance is not aid, and not loans, but medium-term investment that expects a return.[20] A similar instrument, China Asia Fund, was set up by China Eximbank in Asia.

IMPACT ON THE LIVES OF AFRICANS

China's approach to development cooperation clearly offers opportunities, but also entails some risks. The benefits include greater ownership, and more equal partnerships, lower transaction costs, a new emphasis on infrastructure and productive activities, "agency of restraint," and policy space. The risks include the potential for higher costs when contracts are signed without competitive tenders, as well as the lower labor, social, and environmental standards that come with a middle-income developing country partner, as opposed to one at a high level of development.

Ownership. Countries across the developing world have been pressing for more ownership over their aid and development finance. The Chinese have neither the expertise, nor the inclination, nor the personnel to engage in development strategy planning or write country assistance strategies, for any of the countries where they engage. In fact, such an activity would probably never occur to them.

For the Chinese, ownership starts (and sometimes ends) at the top. In cases where leaders do not coordinate with ministries, this can cause problems, as in Liberia where a President asked the Chinese to build a hospital upcountry, leaving the Liberian health ministry scrambling to figure out staffing for the remote location. But governments who do have well thought out development plans appreciate the Chinese willingness to follow their lead. They also appreciate that the Chinese principle of noninterference in internal affairs allows them to maintain sovereignty over their development strategy.

Partnership. The language of "donor" and "recipient" remains widespread in the West, despite the efforts of the Paris Declaration to shift to partnership. As the West has found, it is difficult to have real partnerships when one partner is wealthy and autonomous and the other is poor and dependent. As a Chinese researcher once asked me, "how can you fight poverty and stay in a five star hotel?"

Skilled Africans can't help but wonder why foreign experts who work beside them are earning 10 or 20 times their salaries, all paid out of a foreign aid budget (or even worse, financed by a loan that will later be paid out of African Government workers' taxes). The Chinese live far more simply in Africa, often in group housing or compounds, and share a frugal mentality. The managing director of the Bank of China branch in Lusaka is authorized to fly business class, his assistant told me, but he flies economy class instead "to save the bank money." It is hard to imagine a similar gesture from a World Bank employee.

Lower Transaction Costs. China's tiny aid bureaucracy (70 professionals in MOFCOM's Department of Aid to Foreign Countries, 100 in China Eximbank's Concessional Loan Department) means that the Chinese rarely participate in the stream of donor missions that occupy the time of so many African ministries. China's aid program offers a relatively limited menu of turnkey projects, mainly focused on infrastructure: roads and bridges, telecoms and power plants, sanitation and water systems. Once a project is initiated or requested, all important decisions are made in Beijing, not by the Chinese mission in the host country. Contrary to conventional wisdom, Chinese banks do require environmental impact assessments, but will often accept those prepared by their borrowers. In recent years Chinese banks have begun to require more elaborate environmental impact appraisals for loans. Increasingly, these are contracted out to European firms.

New Emphasis on Infrastructure and Production. Chinese companies and banks appear to be far more open to financing and investing in infrastructure, resource processing activities and industrial projects than their peers coming from Western countries. "Donors have neglected power since the 1990s," a recent study noted, pointing to an infrastructure financing gap of some US$93 billion in Africa.[21] African countries themselves spend some US$45 billion a year on infrastructure; and Chinese companies have been building much of this, earning revenues of over US$20 billion annually from construction and engineering contracts on the continent. Worldwide, over 60 percent of China Eximbank's concessional loans have been committed to infrastructure projects.[22]

After Liberia's war ended, President Johnson Sirleaf repeatedly said that her number one priority was getting roads financed. According to adviser Steven Radelet, "No one was doing it. They all said 'we don't do roads. But the Chinese Ambassador said: 'we'll do roads.' And things changed." [23]

In Ghana, the China Africa Development Fund is one of the equity investors in a joint venture with the Government of Ghana and Bosai Minerals Group in a Sekondi industrial estate that will be anchored by a proposed alumina refinery. Ghana has long been a producer of bauxite, mined by large western firms—Rio Tinto (now merged with Canada-based Alcan), and the U.S. company Alcoa—who refined the bauxite into aluminum ingots which were then shipped out. But none of these partners was willing to invest in building an aluminium industry.

As Ghana's Minister of Trade and Industry put it, the Chinese project "will allow our country to finally achieve our long-term objective of establishing an integrated aluminium industry and make the most of our resources." [24] Business Monitor International predicted that the Sekondi Industrial Freezone would "create a major growth area in West Ghana." [25]

Another Chinese company is building Chad's first petroleum refinery in a 60:40 joint venture. The Chadian Government applied for a preferential export credit to help finance its share of the venture. Although the famous Chad-Cameroon pipeline project supported by the World Bank originally envisaged building a small refinery, this did not happen, and the pipeline instead transferred Chad's crude oil outside, while Chad continued to import all its refined petroleum products. Ngata Ngoulou, Chadian Finance and Budget Minister, said: "If we had made this request to our traditional partners, they would have certainly told us to give up the idea." [26]

Likewise, in Niger, the Chinese approach contrasted with that of earlier Western companies. Some Africans believe that "China's efforts offer opportunity for industrialization on a scale never countenanced by the colonizers of old." [27] Ibrahim Ango, president of Niger's Chamber of Commerce, told a reporter that French oil firm Total and the U.S. firm ExxonMobil both held oil concessions in Niger's Agadem region, but refused to consider refining oil. "East time the government said, 'build a refinery,' they said: 'it's impossible.' The Chinese came and said: 'A refinery? What size?'" [28]

Agency of Restraint. China's system of resource-backed infrastructure loans is a way for countries with weak governance, unable to access global finance, and prone to the "resource curse," to opt for an agency of restraint. With multiple competing demands for access to the revenue streams from their natural resources, leaders find it hard to say no. Commodity-backed loans are a precommitment technique. They allow a government to have public works expenditures today, paying for them with future exports. In weak governments, rather than trying directly to improve the host government's accountability mechanisms, or forcing improvements through conditionality, the Chinese accept that institutional development is a long-term process. They manage their fiduciary responsibility by keeping control over the finances and almost never giving cash. As one African official told me: "with China you never see that money."

Debt Sustainability. China's new ability to offer large-scale finance arrived just as African countries were finally successful in getting multilateral debt relief through the Highly Indebted Poor Countries (HIPC) program. Paris Club and multilateral creditors have worried about a new debt burden. In the DRC, for example, China's initial offer of a credit line of US$6 billion for infrastructure and another US$3 billion or so to finance the copper mine appeared certain to sink the war-ravaged country beneath towering waves of debt just when the government was negotiating with the Paris Club for debt forgiveness on the cold war era loans racked up under Mobutu.

Yet a different way of looking at this package suggests that while the Chinese financing model involves large sums of credit, it also frequently creates new cash flows to finance the investments. When asked about Western criticism of China's African engagement during a press conference at the World Bank/IMF Spring Meetings in April 2011, Ngata Ngoulou, Chad's Finance and Budget Minister, said, regarding debt: "it is more important that the debt burden of African countries is manageable. For us, this is a big difference. Even if the some of the Western critique of China makes sense, I still do not think it a bad thing for Africa. We borrow for our industrialization projects and the debt will be repaid from their profits." [29] This also creates incentives for the Chinese companies and banks to do what they can to ensure that their investments are financially sustainable, an incentive that was often missing in past multilateral debt.

Impact on Local Firms and Workers. Chinese imports, particularly of textiles, have been devastating competition for African firms using outdated technologies to produce for local markets. At the same time, some African entrepreneurs are partnering with Chinese companies or using new Chinese machinery and technical assistance, and competing successfully with Chinese imports into their regions.[30] Indeed, World Bank data shows that between 2004 and 2009, although Chinese imports were rising dramatically, sub-Saharan African countries experienced average annual increases of 3 to 5 percent in manufacturing for every year except 2008, the first year of the global financial crisis.[31] In Ethiopia, Senegal, Sudan, Tanzania, Uganda, Zambia, and Zimbabwe, all large importers of Chinese goods, manufacturing grew by an average of 9 percent in 2009.

In the construction industry, Chinese companies clearly benefit from contracts tied to Chinese finance. When these contracts are delivered without competitive bidding, as in many export credit arrangements, countries may find themselves paying higher costs than would otherwise be the case. Yet even when they have no financial support, Chinese companies are winning a large share of the small and medium construction contracts that might have gone to local firms in the past.

Chinese companies do have low costs but construction firms in Zambia and Namibia have documented unfair Chinese business practices: collusive bidding, low wages, and a tendency to hire contract workers in order to get around mandated labor benefits (paid holidays, sick leave, etc.) for permanent staff. A study by Namibian labor unions pointed out that the Chinese were following the same practices as local African firms. European-owned firms that adhered to local labor laws and regulations suffered most.[32]

Chinese companies do bring a larger proportion of their workforce from home than Western firms, but this is the case mainly for construction projects in oil-rich countries like Algeria, Libya, or Angola where local labor is expensive. In other places, with few exceptions, Chinese projects have a majority of Africans in their workforce. Those who do fieldwork regularly report this reality. For example, a researcher who recently visited Cameroon expecting to find large groups of Chinese workers found instead that every construction site she visited had Cameroonian workers under Chinese managers.[33] It is the poor conditions of this employment, and not its absence, that is a constant complaint among African workers.

Policy Space. Decades of advice and conditionality imposed by the West have pushed African governments to rely on the magic of the marketplace, develop by opening their markets and exporting according to their comparative advantage in raw commodities. While the Washington Consensus usefully stressed key macroeconomic fundamentals—low inflation and adequate foreign reserves—it was skeptical of the kind of industrial policy and targeted intervention practiced across East Asia, and it had little to say about strategic development policy.

The achievements of the Chinese in moving millions out of poverty are recognized as a significant success. But like other East Asian countries, although China moved toward the market, they did it gradually, and in particular, they did not begin by liberalizing trade, as recommended by the Washington Consensus. Their model emphasizes fiscal stability and macroeconomic balance, but also learning and experimentation. The enormity of this example provides policy space for African governments to experiment with other approaches to fostering development.

AFRICAN REACTIONS TO CHINA'S APPROACH

Africans have reacted to China's approach in different ways. Government officials and leaders have largely been very positive, with some exceptions, such as Zambian opposition politician and, now, new President, Michael Sata. Civil society, trade unions, and some sectors of local business have been more wary. This is particularly the case with regard to Chinese labor practices, the influx of small-scale traders, the impact of Chinese goods on local manufacturing, and the fact that by engaging primarily with governments, Chinese aid and export credits reinforce incumbent leaders. Concerns have also been raised about the high levels of counterfeiting and substandard goods coming into Africa from China.

Opposition politicians have sometimes found that Chinese engagement can provide ample fodder for political capital. Writing an op-ed about a large Chinese economic zone planned for Mauritius, Anil Gayan, an opposition member of Parliament, wrote: "It is a voluntary colonization . . . a danger for our security."[34] Michael Sata, a perennial Presidential candidate in Zambia, famously dismissed the Chinese in his country as "infesters" not investors.

Public opinion polls in Africa show that populations there are generally evenhanded about Chinese engagement. In Cameroon, for example:

> . . . 70 percent of the respondents in one poll were "disturbed by the Chinese influx" while at the same time 92 percent in the same survey admitted that China is good for Cameroon's economy. Also, 81 percent welcomed Chinese products, which benefited poorer parts of the population.[35]

A study analyzing Afrobarometer's public opinion surveys in 20 countries found that while most Africans expressed positive views of China's role, Africans who rank human rights as high in importance were more likely to have an unfavorable opinion. Views on the importance of democracy were not correlated with negative opinions of China, however.[36]

Government officials generally express positive views. Speaking at the World Bank/IMF Annual Meeting in April 2011, Dr. Situmbeko Musokotwane, the Zambian Minister of Finance, compared China's business and aid model with that of the West. China used aid and other tools vigorously to encourage its companies to invest in Africa, he said, but that did not seem to be the case for Europe and America, whose aid programs were more paternalistic, and seemed to be designed as charity: "at least help them not to suffer, we can't do much more than that. They're not ready for investment." [37]

Mthuli Ncube, chief economist at the Africa Development Bank, commented in Tunis that the Chinese model "is a fascinating and new model in terms of how aid is flowing into Africa and how infrastructure investment is being conducted and supported." China, he said, is "posing a challenge and making us think about aid architecture, this kind of governance-neutral approach to aid engagement and investment in Africa." China's approach might even be more sustainable, he said. "We can talk forever about Millennium Development Goals but my view is you can only pay for MDGs targets and progress not through aid but through growth." [38]

A survey of African stakeholders carried out in 40 African countries by the OECD for the African Economic Outlook 2011 found that emerging partners such as China were ranked as having a comparative advantage for cooperation in infrastructure, innovation, and even health compared with Africa's traditional bilateral and multilateral partners. Economist Helmut Reisen, head of research at the OECD's Development Center commented: "these results are striking considering all the effort traditional donors have put into these sectors." [39]

STEPS THAT CAN BE TAKEN TO IMPROVE COOPERATION WITH CHINA

First, invest some effort in getting behind the headlines and seeing what China is actually doing. The Chinese have six decades of experience with aid in Africa. They've spent time analyzing their own past failed aid projects, and they've come up with a different model of engagement, much of which does not actually involve official development aid. It's much closer to Japan's pattern of engagement with other Asian countries.

Through diplomatic processes like the Forum on China-Africa Cooperation (FOCAC), initiated in 2000, China has increasingly coordinated its development engagement with Africa on a "whole of government" basis, with involvement by the line ministries (agriculture, health, education, science and technology), universities and think-tanks, policy banks, as well as the ministries of commerce and foreign affairs. This synergy has led to practical experiments based on China's own experience:

- Resource-backed infrastructure loans. Credits that allow countries with poor credit ratings to borrow today and pay with tomorrow's exports.
- Overseas economic zones that encourage Chinese companies to move their labor, energy, and resource-intensive manufacturing offshore.
- A US$5 billion equity fund provides additional capital investment options for suitable Chinese companies in Africa who plan invest in public-private partnerships, joint ventures, and manufacturing.
- A US$1 billion fund to provide loans to African small and medium enterprises, channeled through African countries' national development banks.
- Twenty agro-technology demonstration centers that ask Chinese institutes and agribusinesses to build sustainable business models that can cross-subsidize development outreach with profitable income opportunities.

These tools are for the most part not funded by China's official aid, but they are about development. More importantly, they respond to the requests of Africans for assistance that will help in building infrastructure and creating new jobs. The Chinese approach to development finance in poorer countries demands that we reconsider our assumptions and our neat categories that separate "aid" from business support.

THE EXAMPLE OF HEALTH

China has hosted two International Roundtables on China-Africa Health Collaboration, on December 4–5, 2009, and on February 11–12, 2011, respectively, organized by the Chinese Alliance for South-South Health Cooperation Research, the Peking University Institute for Global Health, and the China Institute of International Studies, and cosponsored by the World Bank Institute, China's MOH, WHO, and the Bill & Melinda Gates Foundation. Interest in collaboration appears to be growing.

However, the lack of understanding and, sometimes, the misrepresentation of the nature of Chinese engagement overseas, have created a challenge for United States-China collaboration. For example, one analyst writes: "More than 2,000 Chinese medical personnel have been sent to Yemen during the past 40 years to assist with Yemen's health and medical programs and responses to disasters. *In exchange,* China has received access to Yemen's markets and energy resources" (emphasis added).[40] Another argues, without evidence, that "Health diplomacy helps pave the way for Chinese oil companies [sic] to win mining rights for oil, platinum, and other natural resources, . . . one part of the quid pro quo that encourages African states to make these concessions and provide Chinese companies access to these resources."[41] It is more accurate and useful to see China's health diplomacy as a broad-based strategy aimed at building goodwill across the continent, no more an "exchange" or "quid pro quo" than U.S. health engagement. To encourage official collaboration between the United States and China in health, high-level support by political leaders on both sides will be necessary to build trust and overcome suspicions like those noted above.

Operationally, the Chinese concern about not intervening in the internal affairs of their partners means that they operate with a great deal of regard for local ownership of their assistance efforts. Therefore, a key step in collaboration requires genuine buy-in by an interested African partner. The stars need to be aligned further: In the partner country, it will be essential to have constructive commitment by both the Chinese and American ambassadors.

A parallel track should involve building relationships by working together in multilateral settings, particularly those endorsed by the U.N. or WHO, or in private or more decentralized settings, for example, foundations with health-related programs in China as well as Africa—the Rockefeller, Ford, or the Gates Foundations. With a "green light" from political officials, experiments in cooperation can be started between organizations such as the Centers for Disease Control in China and in the United States.

Possible areas for collaboration could include not only malaria but also sanitation and rural and urban water supply efforts. The Chinese have extensive experience in building low-cost water supply systems in Africa, whereas the United States could focus on public health education (e.g., promoting hand washing). Some American officials have expressed interest in purchasing more Chinese antimalarial medicines for use in Africa, as long as they are certified by WHO. Assisting Chinese firms to gain WHO certification could be mutually beneficial. Building up the capacity of African governments to test and monitor imported medical products in order to fight substandard and counterfeit drugs would also be useful.[42]

FINAL POINTS

In conclusion let me stress three points: realism versus alarmism; good policy needs good information; engage China multilaterally.

Realism versus Alarmism. China's rise in Africa should be seen in context. China is still a far smaller player than the West. The Chinese Government has much in common with other rising economic powers: Brazil and India, for example. Brazil is also expanding on the continent. The Economist recently reported that Brazil has more embassies in Africa than the U.K., for example. Lack of transparency is also a common pattern for these emerging powers. Brazil, India, and China are alike in not being members of the OECD and in not reporting their aid and development finance flows to the OECD's Development Assistance Committee, which tracks these things on behalf of its members and others. Brazil, India, and China also have similar levels of corruption, according to Transparency International.

Good Policy Needs Good Information. Pushing China to be more transparent about aid and official finance may eventually yield results, and this would be helpful for us in reacting to China's rise. But in the meantime, it is possible to gather better information and to publish that information. In the 1970s, the CIA gathered information on China's aid program and published this information regularly. Today, it appears that no one in the U.S. Government is gathering and sifting through the volumes of information on Chinese engagement. The information that is sometimes made available to Congress, for example, a report on Chinese "aid" written by the Congressional Research Service that estimated annual aid flows from China of some $18 billion in 2007 alone, is not always as careful or accurate as it could be.[43] As a Washington Post article said not long ago, "China is no enemy, but inflating the challenge from China could be just as dangerous as underestimating it."[44]

Engage China Multilaterally. China is a member of the United Nations, World Trade Organization, and the World Bank and International Monetary Fund, the World Health Organization. All of these have rules and norms on global engagement that China has pledged to uphold: rules on export credit subsidies, for example, or on debt sustainability and reporting of international credits. At the same time, China is not a member of the OECD, where many of our rules on trade, investment, export credits and official finance are made. The OECD sets the standard for being a responsible global player (even if the standard is not followed consistently by OECD members). The Chinese by and large are familiar with these rules. We need to think about ways in which we can make actually joining the club—as South Korea and Mexico have recently done—both feasible and attractive to the Chinese.

End Notes

1. This testimony draws on Deborah Brautigam, "The Dragon's Gift: The Real Story of China in Africa," Oxford: Oxford University Press, 2011 (2009) and Deborah Brautigam, "China in Africa: What Can Western Donors Learn?" Norfund, August 2011, http://norfund.no/images/stories/publikasjoner/andre_publikasjoner/Norfund_China_in_Africa.pdf.

2. Ministry of Commerce, "China Commerce Yearbook," Beijing, 2009.

3. OECD, "Development Assistance Committee (DAC) Statistics," http://stats.oecd.org/.

4. USAID, "Congressional Budget Justifications, Foreign Operations, Annex on Regional Operations, Budget Year 2012," http://www.usaid.gov/performance/cbj/158268.pdf.

5. "Global Health Initiative," http://foreignassistance.gov/Initiative_GH_2012.aspx?FY=2012.

6. Brautigam, "Dragon's Gift," 317. The percentage of aid going to Africa is adjusted slightly (from my estimate of 43 percent to the actual figure of 45.7 percent, revealed in State Council, "China's Foreign Aid," Beijing, April 2011. Rapid increases mean annual aid commitments are higher than disbursements.

7. USAID, "USAID Primer: What We Do and How We Do It," Washington, DC, revised January 2006, http://www.usaid.gov/about_usaid/PDACG100.pdf. A small number of additional personnel are seconded from other agencies or institutions.

8. Information Office, "China's Foreign Aid," Beijing, People's Republic of China, State Council, April 2011, 4. Currency conversions are on the basis of the exchange rate in 2009. These totals are not very meaningful, however, as the Chinese figures in RMB yuan were simply aggregated, without accounting for inflation.

9. Martyn Davies, "How China is Influencing Africa's Development," background paper for the "Perspectives on Global Development 2010: Shifting Wealth," April 2010.

10. "Concessional financing," http://www.economics-dictionary.com/definition/concessional-financing.html [accessed June 15, 2011]. Although market rates vary strikingly around the world, this clear, standard definition suggests that the label "concessional" should be applied only for finance that is given below the benchmark rate for the currency in which the loan is issued.

11. China Eximbank, "Annual Report 2010," p. 22. The Chinese figures were RMB 278 billion.

12. China Eximbank, "The Export-Import Bank of China Hosted a Symposium on Financing and Project Cooperation in Africa," news release, July 25, 2007.

13. Deborah Brautigam, "Chinese Aid and African Development," New York: St. Martin's Press, 1998.

14. The United States has the government-owned Export-Import Bank. Germany has a publicly owned bank: KfW, or Kreditanstalt für Wiederaufbau to support exports. Brazil owns BNDES, Banco Nacional de Desenvolvimento Economico e Social (Brazil National Social and Economic Development Bank). China's three policy banks are China Development Bank, China Export Import Bank, and the Agricultural Development Bank of China.

15. Deborah Brautigam and Tang Xiaoyang, "African Shenzhen: China's Special Economic Zones in Africa," Journal of Modern African Studies, 49, 1 (2011): 27–54.

16. For an excellent overview of the various types of financial support available to China's enterprises under "Going Global" see Duncan Freeman, "China's Outward Investments: Challenges and Opportunities for the EU," Brussels Institute of Contemporary China Studies Policy Paper (no date).

17. Institute of Economic and Resource Management, "A Report on the Development of China's Market Economy," Beijing: China Foreign Economic Relations and Trade Publishing House, 2003, 129.

18. Erica Downs, "Inside China, Inc: China Development Bank's Cross-Border Energy Deals," Washington, DC, Brookings, March 2011.

19. People's Daily, April 9, 2000.

20. China-Africa Development Fund, "Online Q & A," http://www.cadfund.com/en/ques_on line.asp?Id=9 [accessed June 29, 2011].

21. Vivien Foster and Cecilia Briceno-Garmendia, eds. "Africa's Infrastructure: A Time for Transformation," Agence Francaise de Developpement and the World Bank, 2010, p. 8.

22. Information Office of the State Council, "China's Foreign Aid," Beijing, China, April 2011, p. 6.

23. Steve Radelet, Meeting at Center for Global Development, October 9, 2007.

24. Hanna S. Tetteh, Statement Read on Behalf of Government at a Press Conference," October 26, 2011.

25. "Oil Exports to Propel Growth Boom," Africa Monitor, v. 12, n. 8, August 2011, p. 7.

26. "CNPC and Chadian government sign MOU on financing for N'Djamena Refinery," Press Release China National Petroleum Company, August 25, 2009, http://www.cnpc.com.cn/en/press/

newsreleases/CNPCandChadiangovernmentsignMOUonfinancingforNDjamenaRefinery__.htm [accessed July 15, 2011].

27. Burgis, "A Richer Seam."

28. Burgis, "A Richer Seam."

29. IMF, Video of Press Briefing, African Ministers, World Bank/IMF Spring Meetings, April 16, 2011, http://www.imf.org/external/mmedia/view.aspx?vid=907396692001 [accessed July 30, 2011].

30. See Brautigam, "The Dragon's Gift," for the success stories of several African entrepreneurs.

31. World Bank, World Development Indicators. Analysis covers all sub-Saharan African countries with data between 2004–2009.

32. J. Anthony Yaw Baah and Herbert Jauch (ed.), "Chinese Investments in Africa: A Labour Perspective," African Labour Research Network, Windhoek, Namibia, May 2009.

33. Lisa Sodalo, "China in Cameroon's Construction Sector: Towards Enforcement of Higher Labour Standards Than Local Regulation?," China Monitor, May 2011, http://www.ccs.org.za/wp-content/uploads/2011/06/China_Monitor_MAY_2011SG1.pdf [accessed June 28, 2011].

34. Brautigam, "The Dragon's Gift."

35. Max Rebol, "Alternatives: Turkish Journal of International Relations," Vol. 9, No. 4, Winter 2010.

36. Aleksandra Gadzala and Marek Hanusch, "African Perspectives on China in Africa: Gauging Popular Perceptions and Their Economic and Political Determinants," Afrobarometer Working Paper No. 117, January 2010.

37. Comments at a panel, Washington, DC, April 15, 2011.

38. Ndamu Sandu, "Chinese Aid to Africa in the Spotlight," The Standard, November 29, 2010.

39. Helmut Reisen, "Emerging Partners Create Policy Space for Africa," Shifting Wealth Blog, June 6, 2011. The traditional partners were thought to have a comparative advantage for exports and for governance.

40. Denise Zheng, "China's Use of Self Power," in Chinese Soft Power, ed. McGiffert, 4.

41. Jeremy Youde, "China's Health Diplomacy in Africa," China: An International Journal 9, no. 1 (2011): 159, 160.

42. See the discussion by Liu Youfa, "Responsibilities of China and the United States in Promoting Global Health Programs in Africa," paper presented at CSIS-China Institute of International Studies Conference Conference, Beijing, May 24, 2011.

43. See, for example, http://www.fas.org/sgp/crs/row/R40361.pdf and my comments on it on my blog: http://www.chinaafricarealstory.com/2010/02/billions-in-aid.html.

44. http://www.washingtonpost.com/wp-dyn/content/article/2010/02/26/AR2010022602601.html ?sub=AR.

Senator COONS. Thank you very much, Dr. Brautigam.

Mr. Hayes, if you would.

STATEMENT OF STEPHEN HAYES, PRESIDENT AND CEO, THE CORPORATE COUNCIL ON AFRICA, WASHINGTON, DC

Mr. HAYES. Thank you.

It is very good to see all four of you.

Senator COONS. Turn your mike on.

Mr. HAYES. Sorry. Good to see all four of you. And certainly, Senator Lugar, it is great to see you again as well.

I would like to speak really more from the private sector point of view, of course, and as I noted in my written testimony, I am honored to be invited to provide testimony.

Much of my life has been built around both China and Africa relations with the United States, and certainly, currently, the status as president of the Corporate Council on Africa has brought together my interest in both regions of the world.

For the Corporate Council on Africa, this issue is of high urgency. It is nearly 200 companies represent about 85 percent of all United States foreign direct investment in Africa. As we attempt to expand United States trade with and investment in Africa, the relationship with China becomes increasingly important to the American economy.

China's interests in Africa do go beyond economic and include wider political influence on a global scale, as does ours. In the global marketplace, China is and will continue to be an aggressive competitor to the United States and other nations, including those in Africa.

They have every right to be such. No one should challenge China's right to be engaged in Africa. Both China and the nations of Africa are free to seek any and all trading partners.

Neither is China alone in increasing its investment in Africa. The emerging economies of Brazil, Russia, India, South Africa as a group are outpacing United States investment in Africa.

However, China does enjoy certain advantages over the United States and other nations, particularly following rules and practices of the OECD. Those rules forbid bribery of public officials in any form, as well as eliminating predatory practices on export credit financing.

Chinese counterfeit goods have flooded African markets, not only undercutting United States companies who have created the products—some of the products—driving them out of the market, but also creating health risk with counterfeit medicines. International patent rights are ignored, and this has implications for supporting development of new products and manufacturing in Africa, as well as exporting nations.

Chinese populations are also increasing throughout Africa, with major socioeconomic implications for the continent. While this is the business of African host nations and China, it does bring up questions of future stability of nations, as well as create questions around the use of local versus imported labor.

The United States strategy toward China should be twofold. The U.S. Government should do more to help American companies compete in Africa. Far greater United States private sector engagement in Africa will not only help African development but will also help rebuild the manufacturing base in America.

Our aid program should be shifted toward building a vibrant private sector throughout Africa, and USAID should recognize the United States private sector as a partner in African development. I think our competitive advantage in this regard will be if we can compete and work with a vibrant private sector in Africa, then private sector to private sector is more in our line, and we can develop that. I think that is one of the emphasis that we should be placing.

In this regard, many of our members' experiences and insights are reflected in legislation being developed by Senator Durbin that may make it possible for U.S. companies to compete on a more even playing field. We should recognize, however, that China will be a long-term player in Africa and that China offers an opportunity also for America in terms of economic partnerships.

Cooperation will require time and the establishment of trust, but there are some business partnerships already between the United States and China in Africa. But there are also areas that Professor Shinn rightly noted that we can now cooperate in, such as South Sudan and the Horn of Africa.

Much of this cooperation, though, will be built through joint ventures in the United States. If the United States and China can find common ground in Africa, not only will the United States-China relationship strengthen but so, too, will the benefit to Africa. In this regard, the Corporate Council on Africa will be leading a delegation of businesses to China in February to meet on possible cooperation in Africa.

Thank you.

[The prepared statement of Mr. Hayes follows:]

PREPARED STATEMENT OF STEPHEN HAYES

Senator Kerry and other members of the Foreign Relations Subcommittee on African Affairs, I am honored to be asked to testify before you on China's role in Africa. I have worked for some years with Chinese emerging leaders before I became President of the Corporate Council on Africa more than 12 years ago. Much of my life has been engaged in China and African affairs.

The Corporate Council on Africa, whom I proudly serve, is a membership organization of more than 180 companies. Collectively the members represent more than 85 percent of all U.S. private sector direct investment in Africa. Probably no organization in America is more engaged in the economic and political landscape of Africa. As such we are a nonprofit, nonlobbying organization committed to increasing U.S.-Africa trade and investment. We are engaged in different ways in most issues affecting the economic relationship. Certainly, the Chinese engagement with Africa is one of those key issues.

A great deal has been said about China's perceived domination of the African market. Clearly China has long-term aims, both economic and political, through its heightened involvement in Africa. Given their needs for the development of their own nation coupled with the fact that so much of the world's strategic resources are to be found in Africa this should not be surprising. I think it wise to presume that their interests go beyond just economic, however, and they seek wider political influence than they have had in the past. They are, after all, one of the principal bankers for the world right now, and their planning, unlike most countries today, is cohesive, coherent, and long-term, both in economics and politics.

In global business, contracts are completed when three basic dynamics are realized: capacity to deliver, decisionmaking and execution of the contract itself. In capacity to deliver and in execution of the contract, that is the completion of the product, the United States can evenly compete with China or any other nation in the world. However, the decisionmaking process, which affects the time that a contract can be completed, is far less cumbersome in China than it is in the USA. Nearly every U.S. deal relies on private investors, and on this matter China has a distinct advantage.

The decisionmaking process in China is far more efficient than it is in the United States. Decisions and recommendations for investment are often directed by the government, or at the very least, and they are able to meet requests from African governments far more quickly than we can in this country. There are far more checks and balances that most business deals must meet in our own system. We also operate our economic models on business-to-business contracts, while many African countries, especially those with weak private sectors, operate on Government-to-business model, more similar to the Chinese model than to the American model. The competitive advantage clearly goes to China under these circumstances.

It is not necessarily China's capacity, or even its ability to execute/complete contracts quickly that defines its competitive advantage in Africa. The West still holds key advantages in both technological and scientific capacity, as well as in management skills and probably quality of workmanship. Rather it is the Chinese ability to forge consensus and mobilize resources quickly that gives them a distinct advantage in the African marketplace.

No one should challenge China's right to be engaged in Africa. Their involvement has helped Africa perhaps more than any nation has helped Africa in any 10-year period directly and indirectly. Certainly, the China engagement with Africa has brought about heightened interest in Africa. Infrastructure has expanded in many countries thanks to Chinese investment and political interests. More productive agriculture has been developed in some countries where China is active, and certainly the increased competition for strategic minerals has driven up the price of commodities and raised national incomes for many African countries.

It is not China alone, however, that is increasing its investment in Africa. While it can be debated whether the increased interest of China in Africa has spurred on other nations to become more engaged economically in Africa, the combined investment of the so-called BRICS (Brazil, Russia, India, China, and South Africa) has surpassed all U.S. investment in Africa. As a result, the economies of these countries have also shown greater strength and stability in these times than most developed nations. There are growing investment flows into Africa from the Middle East, ranging from Turkey to the nations of Arabian Peninsula and to Iran. We also see growing interest in Africa from Japan, particularly since its recent nuclear disaster, but also because of the growing influence of China. China's interest and growing involvement in Africa is perhaps one of the most important political and economic phenomena in the world right now, and in my view, the United States has been very slow to either understand its meaning and ramifications for our own country and its own economic and political future.

It is difficult to know exactly how much China is investing in Africa, and it is just as difficult to pin down exactly how they are winning the competition. Their currency is artificially pegged so exact values are almost impossible to determine. Certainly, their government and their private sector are working closely together, and the Chinese Government appears to help its private sector investing in Africa as no other government helps its own private sector. Some of this is due to the history of China, particularly over the last 30 years, and some is simply due to the fact that China can underbid most projects through lower labor costs and through government-subsidized assistance to Chinese companies. While Chinese companies win infrastructure contracts with low bids and subsidized financing, they also have developed a reputation for limited employment for Africans, limited technological transfer, and in some cases, uneven workmanship. If Chinese companies do not correct these practices, it presents an opportunity for American companies to win contracts and train Africans during project implementation, which is in Africa's long-term benefit. One American company, Symbion Power, has done exactly that in winning an MCC-funded contract for power transmission in Tanzania. It also partnered with CCA to develop an HIV/AIDS prevention campaign for its employees in Tanzania.

What is also obvious is that the Chinese population on the African Continent is increasing in nearly every nation. Chinese businesses are sprouting up in not only the major cities of Africa but in smaller urban areas as well. Chinese laborers are brought in with Chinese construction projects, and it is difficult to determine if the laborers return to China after the projects are completed. In many areas, the Chinese appear to be permanent immigrants. Again, exact figures are difficult to obtain, but I have traveled to no African country where some citizens of the country did not express concern about the growing Chinese domination of the local markets and their influence in displacing African workers on construction projects and in new businesses. In the recent Presidential elections in Zambia, the growing Chinese influence over the economy was the key political issue. One should not be surprised if similar issues develop in other countries on the continent.

Clearly, the Chinese have no interest in following OECD rules. They are not members of OECD and therefore are not constrained by the rules in their negotiations with the governments and businesses of Africa. They are, in many ways, at a distinct competitive advantage over its Western counterparts, as are other countries not bound by OECD rules and regulations. However, again, exactly how the Chinese compete for contracts is not easily verified. There is no requirement for transparency in negotiations and the terms of the contracts are often held privately by the governments and companies involved in the negotiations. I do not think this likely to change in the near future. What is clear, however, is that such tactics have slowed the pace of reform in Africa and strengthened the intransigence of those resisting democratic reform for the benefit of the people.

For U.S. companies, as well as those of other nations, counterfeit goods have flooded the African markets, not only undercutting those who have created the original products, and driving them out of the market, but also creating health risks with counterfeit medicines and false products, with the Africans once again the victims of this exploitation. International patent rights are ignored.

The question before this body is whether China will become so dominant in its control of the African market that this dominance will significantly impair our own policies toward Africa, and whether, in fact, our own need for strategic resources, including fuel, will be threatened. After all, countries will necessarily gravitate toward those countries who are most heavily and directly invested in them. If the United States continues to fail to develop private sector-led growth, can we realistically expect to maintain the same respect and relationships with the African people and the nations of Africa?

Perhaps an even more salient question is what opportunities for jobs in America are never created because American business may be more a spectator than an actor in the African marketplace. It is not a matter of how many jobs are lost, but how many are never created because we have failed to engage in Africa to the same extent others have, particularly as China makes Africa in its highest strategic interests? China's engagement in Africa puts them at the planning tables for nearly all new projects and opportunities. How many jobs are we not creating by not being engaged in Africa?

There are some in this country, (and I hear this from some of our member companies involved in Africa), who believe that it is almost impossible to compete with the Chinese. I do not accept this and think that if we do not compete more effectively in Africa our long-term interests and hopes, as well as our national economy, will suffer sufficiently as to render us a mid-level economy over this century. I believe that our political and economic engagement with Africa is in our highest national interests.

Our strategy as it regards China in Africa should be twofold: we need to find ways to compete, certainly, and I also believe it is in the interests of China, the United States, and the nations of Africa that we find ways to more effectively cooperate.

First, in terms of competition, we should not isolate China as the primary competitor. It is certainly the largest, but as I noted earlier, many other nations are now becoming far more engaged in China, and the economic environment is becoming increasingly competitive. We need to look at our own economic stance toward Africa, regardless of whom we perceive as primary competition. The fact is that we have not shown the same competitive strengths as others, and we need to ask ourselves what needs to be done.

We need to expand and strengthen the ability of American companies to make investment decisions. We need to engage our university systems in more economic research in Africa. Our business schools need to focus more on developing markets globally, just as American companies need to conduct more on-the-ground research in Africa. A company will not invest in Africa if they doubt their ability to recover their investment. Therefore, making investment decisions rests with the quality and the research that provides confidence in long-term sustainability and profitability of investment.

We should recognize that the development goals of Africa do not simply benefit Africa, but are essential to our own national economic security. Private sector-led development throughout Africa will bring about a growing middle class, create greater stability throughout the continent, and provide for U.S. businesses stronger and more reliable business partners. Our traditional approach to development needs to be reexamined and altered to make private sector economic development among our highest priorities.

Second, we need to examine specific barriers to U.S. companies ability to compete more effectively in Africa. There are several serious barriers, largely self-imposed, that hamper our ability to compete.

One such barrier is access to financial markets. Few U.S. banks will finance U.S. companies seeking to do business in Africa, and our own agencies designed to mitigate such risks, such as the Ex-Im Bank have fallen woefully short in addressing the problem. We can provide one example after another of good U.S. projects in Africa failing to get necessary government support. While I think Ex-Im is attempting to address the problem, as is OPIC, the support provided U.S. companies is far below the level of support that the Chinese counterparts provide for their private sector companies seeking to do business in Africa.

A second impediment for U.S. companies doing business in Africa is the necessity to find partnerships. One simply cannot do business easily in Africa without having a reliable partner on the ground. There is no mechanism set up that allows us to easily find a partner. We have a limited number of U.S. Commercial offices in Africa and under budget constraints those that we do have are being closed. These closures are coming at exactly the wrong time. They come when China and others are increasing their commercial government presence throughout the continent. Among the highest priorities of Chinese Embassies is to support its business development in Africa.

At the Corporate Council on Africa we have developed through the support of the U.S. Agency for International Development a U.S.-Africa Business Center whose primary purpose is to identify business partners in Africa for U.S. companies, especially small and medium-sized businesses wishing to do business. It is the only such organization in America and it can only meet a small proportion of the need. This operation needs to be significantly expanded and duplicated in other parts of the country. China provides support for its small businesses investing in Africa. We do very little of this, and as a result hurt our own economy as well as fail to help develop the private sector in Africa.

Diplomatically, I believe that our current Assistant Secretary of State, Johnnie Carson, deserves a great deal of praise for insisting that many of our new ambassadors selected for African posts have significant economic experience. The challenges in Africa are now as much economic as they are political, and traditional diplomacy is no longer applicable to this rapidly changing economic environment.

To his credit, he is also working with U.S. companies to see that they win contracts in Africa. The Department of State and the Corporate Council on Africa are jointly working together now to take a delegation of U.S. power companies to Africa in the first quarter of 2012. The delegation may be lead by Assistant Secretary Carson. The purpose of the mission will be to significantly increase the involvement of U.S. power companies in the development of the power sector in Africa. Few projects could be more important to Africa, as there is not a country on the continent that is meeting its current power needs, and until they do we cannot expect rapid economic development in Africa. This is but one example of how U.S. companies can make a difference to Africa as well as buttress the economy of the United States of America.

At the same time as we increase our competiveness for a share of the African market, I also strongly believe that we must find ways to cooperate with China in Africa. The stakes for humanity are too high for us not to cooperate. While we must recognize that we must compete internationally with China and others if we are to heal our own economic wounds, we must also recognize that partnerships globally must be developed.

In a world facing growing food shortages, water scarcity, climate change, and the social instabilities they cause, any responsible path forward must rely on international cooperation. Yet today we find the United States and China, competitors at the best of times, struggling to resolve how to address their common interests in Africa, a continent that has suffered more than any other in recent centuries from disasters both natural and man-made.

If the United States and China can find common ground in Africa, both Africa and U.S-China relations can make dramatic strides forward. But the challenge is to convince all the actors to put the health and wealth of the global community above national interests, a difficult and rare endeavor.

It is ironic that as we face new global crises, the competition for economic and political advantage is occurring, as it has throughout human history, in Africa, where mankind's struggle for survival first began. Africa offers the arable land needed to provide food for a hungry world; it offers the water to feed the world and quench the thirst of billions, and it offers the remaining minerals necessary to maintain a modern global society. And the primary players competing over African hearts, minds, and resources today are the Americans and the Chinese, with China having the early advantage of money for investment and a plentiful worker supply for export to the continent.

But it is not just the United States and China with an interest in Africa. The Gulf States, Russia, India, and Europe are all looking to Africa as well to feed their people, with the African peoples themselves struggling to control their own destinies and put food on their tables. Africa matters, and the United States and China are going to play an outsized role in Africa's future. But they need to find common ground and lead together. Partnerships of all kinds are needed for Africa's development, and our own economic self-interests.

There can be better days ahead for Africa. Infrastructure development is moving at a rate unseen before, but the needs are still great. No African country has a sufficient power supply to meet current needs, let alone the projected needs of the future. Famine has returned, if it ever really left, to the Horn of Africa, and water is scarce for a large percentage of the continent's population.

Together, the United States and China can lead the world into a more cooperative arrangement, beginning in Africa. They cannot do so without the support of Africans, but they remain, at this moment in history, the two nations most able to develop a stronger Africa, and a more harmonious world. It is not a case for bipolarity. It is simply recognition of history at this particular moment. Someone must lead and right now, the United States cannot lead alone.

Cooperation comes a step at a time. There must be some confidence and trust-building. A project or projects will need to be agreed upon and the host country must be a party to all agreements.

There are several opportunities for the United States and China to cooperate economically in support of both mutual and continental benefit. For example, economic cooperation in South Sudan is to the advantage of both the United States and China. A peaceful and developed South Sudan clearly benefits the interests of China, which has made enormous investments into the oil sector, and would build up a pocket of political stability in an otherwise very tough neighborhood for the United States. The United States and China both have interests in promoting stability in the Horn of Africa. Consistent supply lines and agriculture development is important to both nations, and the Horn of Africa could be one of several future global breadbaskets providing Africa with increased economic power and a better quality-of-life.

Closer cooperation between China and the United States is not something to be feared, but welcomed, by Africa. Such cooperation would bring about greater stability in reality and perception, and would lead to the opening of new markets and a faster influx of new investment into Africa. The sign of two great nations cooperating in and with Africa would be a very positive and welcoming sign of stability and promise for new investors.

Competition is inevitable, but competition does not preclude cooperation. Instead, a cooperative effort to build Africa through amicable competition and cooperation can lead to improved development across the continent, and can lead to far greater understanding for all parties. If the United States and China choose to cooperate in their efforts in Africa, and always include African leaders and the African peoples in the process, they will set the tone for every other nation, and point Africa toward a brighter future.

What we need now is for the leaders in the United States and China to find the courage necessary to seek common ground and elevate international development among its highest priorities.

Senator COONS. I would like to thank all three of our witnesses. And I will begin a first round of 7-minute questions, if I might.

First, Mr. Hayes, let me just follow up on your concluding point. Given the trends shown in the charts and in your testimony, all three of you, what specific policy recommendations would you make for U.S. Government action that would make American business more competitive with regard to China, and what are the areas that you see we might really have some potential for cooperation?

Mr. HAYES. I think there are several areas. One is the Export-Import Bank. I think it has played a less than stellar role in supporting United States business in Africa. I think there are attempts to change that, but certainly, legislation as well as a cultural change within Ex-Im Bank, I think, is required.

The amount that the Chinese Ex-Im Bank supports its own businesses—and China does have a private sector—is phenomenally higher by many times than the United States support of its businesses. It can make decisions quickly.

Ex-Im Bank, as is well documented, takes a long time to make decisions. It hurts American business. We can give you one horror story after another. I won't go into that unless pressed.

I think USAID should shift its development toward the private sector and, again, toward developing the private sector in Africa. Most of its work is in other areas. I think that it could help a great deal in developing the private sector.

If we can develop a middle class, these countries are going to be far more stable. We are going to have more reliable business partners. I also think that we ought to be linking more with business organizations in Africa.

In terms of cooperation, certainly China and the United States has common interest in seeing South Sudan as a stable area. So, certainly, that is one area.

The second area is those areas where our companies can cooperate, where China may be lacking certain areas—we have seen General Electric cooperate with Chinese companies in Africa. So there are those areas of cooperation, particularly on infrastructure.

The reality is that it is to our advantage to work with Chinese companies, as well as others, because they have an advantage already, and it is a way of getting more active in China and Africa.

Senator COONS. Thank you.

Ambassador Shinn, you mentioned in your testimony that African states under pressure from the United States and from the

West to improve their governance practices or their human rights record are less likely to do so when they know they can rely on China for support, and you cited, I think, Zimbabwe and Sudan, among others.

Has China's economically driven aid policy undermined United States policy goals in terms of promoting democracy and human rights and good governance? And is there any evidence that China's increased investment in political engagement may empower or entrench undemocratic or repressive regimes, first?

And then, second, what do you see as the long-term benefit broadly for the average African of the increased Chinese investment engagement in Africa? Has it succeeded in fighting poverty? What is its impact on the ground?

And then, Dr. Brautigam, if you would address those same two questions, please?

Ambassador SHINN. I think the short answer to your question, Senator, is that, yes, Chinese involvement in Africa has, to some degree, undermined Western goals generally of trying to improve democratization, good governance, and human rights.

I don't think that was the intention of Chinese policy. It is just that they have a different philosophical approach to dealing with countries around the world than does the United States.

And having said that, there are sometimes inconsistencies with U.S. policies. I could identify a couple of African countries that are very autocratic, while the United States has not done much in order to try to improve the human rights situation.

But in terms of Chinese policy, it is across the board. It is a policy of aid without political conditions, investment without political conditions, other than the One China Principle, and that is just not the way the United States approaches the situation.

The two major examples are those that I cited earlier, Zimbabwe and Sudan. There are others that don't stand out quite as much as those two countries. But even a country like Ethiopia, for example, where the United States has very good relations, on the one hand would like at the same time to see better human rights practices.

And because Ethiopia has a very strong relationship with China, it is fairly easy for Ethiopia to say, wait a minute, we know where we can get additional help if we need it. Of course, the United States also has other concerns in Ethiopia in terms of its policy. But it does certainly complicate the ability of the United States to pursue an improvement in human rights policies and practices and good governance.

In terms of China's investment in the continent and its impact on the long term, I think I would have to basically give them a positive response to that. They have, indeed, gone heavily into infrastructure, but they have done that because that is precisely what the Africans have requested.

The Africans were requesting an improvement in infrastructure at a time when the West had basically opted out. Angola is a classic example. Following the civil war in Angola at the beginning of this century, when it came to an end, the Angolans wanted the West to come in, invest a lot of money, rebuild their infrastructure. And the West essentially said, no, we are really not that interested.

They went to China, and China said it would be more than happy to do it. Of course, China expected Angola to pay back these loans by sending oil to China. And by the way, China said it has some really good Chinese companies that will build all of these projects for you, and it even has a component of Chinese labor that will come and help to construct the projects.

So it was certainly a good deal for China, but China was the only country that was offering to do this sort of thing. And in the final analysis, if the African countries don't have much improved infrastructure, they are never going to improve their economies. They cannot continue at the level that they were at, say, 10 years ago in terms of infrastructure.

In that sense, China has done them a favor. I think across the board, the effort that China has done to invest on the continent, with some exceptions, has generally been a plus.

Senator COONS. Dr. Brautigam.

And I am about out of time for my first round. So what impact has it had on the United States sort of values agenda to have an expansive Chinese presence on the continent?

Dr. BRAUTIGAM. Thank you.

I just did a paper on this recently, and I actually looked empirically at this. And there is no evidence across the continent that political rights and freedoms have declined in general between 2000 and the present. And in countries where Chinese engagement is larger, there is also no evidence that there has been any systematic impact on human rights or political liberties and freedoms.

So we have an impression that there has been a negative impact, and I think it largely comes from the case of Sudan and Zimbabwe, where the impact has been negative. But by and large, I don't think we see that it has been negative across the continent.

And we can see this with examples that are quite recent. In Sudan, when the countries negotiated a breakup and they had a referendum to enshrine that in law, the Chinese sent referendum monitors rather than trying to fight to keep the two parts of Sudan together.

We can see this in Guinea, where there was a coup and people thought that the Chinese presence there was going to make it so that they wouldn't have a new election to bring in a new government. And that didn't happen. So they had an election, the most free election they have had in their history—although it wasn't perfect.

So we can see this in Zambia, where the leader that was quite heavily favored by the Chinese did not win the election, and they have moved smoothly into a relationship with someone that was quite opposed to their presence. So I think, by and large, they are moving in a less negative direction than we usually think.

In terms of impact, I would add to what Professor Shinn said that I see a lot of interest in manufacturing investment and a lot of people being employed by Chinese companies. This is, again, counter to the conventional wisdom that they don't hire Africans.

The longer a Chinese company is present in Africa, the more the proportion of labor they hire tends to be African, and this makes economic sense for them. And so, what we can find is that the problem is not that they do not hire local people, but treating them well. And they do not generally treat them at the level an American company would. Labor standards, protection and safety standards, all of these are generally abysmal by our standards, and they are roughly at the level that they are in China.

Senator COONS. Thank you very much, Doctor.

Senator Isakson.

Senator ISAKSON. Thank you, Mr. Chairman.

I think Ambassador Shinn's last comments regarding China making the investment and infrastructure and the West backing away from a lot of that points me to what Stephen Hayes said, which I have observed. We need to do a better job as a government of facilitating United States competitive business investing in Africa.

China and business—the line between business with China and China's businesses are kind of blurred, but they are quite clear in the United States. And I know I have been to Equatorial Guinea, where Marathon built the gas liquification facility, which really has transformed economic development in that country.

What kind of things do we need to do, from your perspective, Mr. Hayes, to more facilitate United States business investment from our government's standpoint in Africa?

Mr. HAYES. In addition to what I already said in response to Senator Coons is I also think that we need a far stronger commercial presence among our embassies and our government on Africa. We are cutting back our commercial offices now, at exactly the wrong time. We are actually diminishing our presence on Africa and our commercial offices.

Second, as I mentioned in my paper, the written testimony, I think at least Johnnie Carson should be praised by putting more emphasis on economic knowledge by ambassadors because we are beyond traditional diplomacy. If we are going to be able to compete and strengthen our own political interest in Africa, our embassies here are going to have to be far more attuned to economic realities.

So I think that there needs to be far greater emphasis on that. Those are two things that I think could be done right away.

Senator ISAKSON. In other words, do a better job through our embassies and our ambassadors of promoting U.S. investment by private sector companies.

Mr. HAYES. Certainly that and certainly a greater support of the private sector nationally. We need national leadership to tell the American people why Africa is important. I don't think that has been explained.

Senator ISAKSON. Very good.

Dr. Brautigam, I want you to—you were talking so quickly. I can't write as fast as you were talking, and you made a great statement about realism versus alarmism with regard to China and America's perspective. And I think what I heard you say is we should be realistic to understand China is a lot like Africa. It is still a developing country. Did I hear that right?

Dr. BRAUTIGAM. Yes.

Senator ISAKSON. And so, we should not be alarmed by what they are trying to do. Tell me what the alarmism part was.

Dr. BRAUTIGAM. Thank you for your question.

The alarmism—the realism is that China's rise in Africa needs to be seen in context, that it is a far smaller player than the West. Although some dimensions of engagement, such as investment or trade, can be quite large compared to any one Western country, by and large, China's engagement is far smaller than the West combined.

And they have a lot in common with other rising economic powers. So I think it is unhelpful sometimes to single them out as "the Chinese have low labor standards" or "the Chinese have a lot of corruption." This is true in general of India, Brazil, and the other emerging market players that are also operating in Africa and also a challenge to us.

So this is a common set of problems, and I think it is helpful to address them in common. I think this would be helpful for our diplomacy as well.

Senator ISAKSON. Both you and Ambassador Shinn referred to China vis-a-vis the Sudan, and I don't know which one of you said it. One of you said that Sudan is a real option for China. Whoever said that, would you amplify on that?

Ambassador SHINN. Sure, I would be happy to, Senator.

I think that you have a situation in Sudan today, both North Sudan, the Khartoum Government, and South Sudan, or the Juba Government, where both of these regimes, if they don't make a lot of changes for the positive soon, are on track for becoming failed states. That is often said about North Sudan, which is the case. It is not often said about South Sudan.

Neither country wants that to happen, and neither China nor the United States wants that to happen. There is a mutual interest in both China and the United States to see the comprehensive peace agreement achieve success, to ensure that there is a good relationship between the north and the south.

All of the oil infrastructure for exporting and refining oil is located in the north. Seventy-five percent of the oil is now in the south, and probably most new finds of oil are in the south.

For the time being, the south has no option other than sending that oil out through the north and using northern refineries. Therefore, they are still basically joined at the hip, and they cannot allow—and China and the United States cannot allow them to let this situation break down into some sort of conflict again.

I think it is an ideal situation for the two countries and others, not just China and the United States, to try to work with both Juba and Khartoum to ensure that the CPA works. In a sense, you could argue that China has even greater interest here than the United States does because China built and owns much of the oil infrastructure in the northern part of Sudan.

Senator ISAKSON. Well, you have made a critical point. The CPA is critical in the short-term interest of the United States, and I am glad to hear your observation about China as well, making sure the comprehensive peace agreement works and these countries don't separate.

Not only is it critical on the oil infrastructure, but they border close to proximity to Kenya and Somalia. And you just have an expansion of what is already a bad situation in Somalia and in

Northern Kenya, and it could blow up like a powder keg if you got back in a civil war situation again.

Do you know if our Embassy and our State Department are doing enough to reach out to the Chinese to try and partner in ways to keep the CPA together?

Ambassador SHINN. I don't know, Senator. I am not in Government now. So I am not privy to that kind of information.

I have no doubt that there are contacts. I have visited Khartoum in the last 5 years, met with both the Chinese and the American Embassies. At that time, there was some contact. It was not as great as I would have liked to have seen, but that was a number of years ago.

Mr. HAYES. Just to add to that because it is germane. Princeton Lyman, our emissary, has been to China to discuss Sudan, recently. In fact, I talked to him while he was in China on South Sudan.

Senator ISAKSON. This is one of the great points to come from this hearing. I think it would be incumbent on Senator Coons and myself to engage Princeton or the State Department at a meeting to make sure we are following up on this because I think it is a very cogent point.

Thank you all for your testimony.

Senator COONS. Thank you, Senator Isakson.

Senator Cardin.

Senator CARDIN. Well, first, Mr. Chairman, thank you very much for holding this hearing.

I think this is an extremely important area for us to explore. Obviously, we need to do a better job ourselves in our relationships with Africa on trade. I am proud of my own State of Maryland, that we have established an African trade office with the help, by the way, of the Federal Government and the Small Business Administration.

We have natural ties between many of the countries in Africa and the business community, particularly in the Washington suburban areas. And we have built on that and have built relationships that I think will be very beneficial for business growth here in America but also will help develop the African economy, which is so critically important for stability and for a market for United States goods.

I think that is the most important thing we can do is enhance our own relationship with the continent of Africa.

I want to ask a question, though, of concern to me about China and Africa. China is interested in their own goals and has very little concern about the governance issues in the countries that they deal with, at least that is the impressions that I have.

When we deal with particularly foreign assistance, we deal with issues such as conditionality, making sure that women's rights are protected, dealing with transparency. And with Senator Lugar, we worked on the extractive industries transparency, which is a big issue with dealing with the resource not being a curse, but an advantage to a country. And Africa certainly is a continent that is very much involved in those issues. We deal with anticorruption issues.

And I guess my question to you is, Is there an indication that China's participation in Africa has been a negative influence on those issues, such as advancement of women's rights, transparency, anticorruption, those types of issues? Have we seen any indication that China's involvement offers an avenue for some of the repressive regimes to get the type of commerce they need without having to deal with the conditionality of Western powers?

Ambassador SHINN. Senator, I would be happy to respond to that. I addressed—it might have been just before you arrived—the connection between human rights and democratization and the Chinese impact. My take on it is that although not intentionally, it does have a negative influence on the American desire to see better human rights practices on the continent.

If you take specifically, however, women's rights and corruption—in fact, if you break this down into various topics—it becomes a more nuanced situation. I don't see any negative impact in Africa of China's activities on women's rights, for example. If it is there, I just haven't observed it.

Corruption traditionally has been a problem. I also see some changes in how China deals with corruption. I think, increasingly, China is finding that that is not the best way to do business around the world and that it is costing them, too. And I see a willingness to rethink the whole concept of engaging in corruption.

So China is not there yet, but at least I think the trend is in the right direction. I think you have to break these all down into their individual issues, and there will be some areas where Chinese influence is not helpful. There will be others where it is essentially neutral and even a couple where it might be helpful.

Corporate social responsibility is one where China is beginning to show an interest in improving its policies in Africa and around the world, as it is doing in China. I think that is a potential cooperative area with the United States, where we have a much better record on corporate social responsibility. I think China is willing to be more helpful on that issue.

Senator CARDIN. Do you see any indication that China is importing technology into Africa that could be used to repress human rights advances, such as cell phone jamming or Internet access or that type of technology, which China certainly has used in its own country? Is that being exported to Africa by repressive regimes?

Ambassador SHINN. There is some indication of that. It definitely occurred in Zimbabwe a number of years ago. Even in Ethiopia, where China has been deeply involved in the communications sector, Ethiopia has a very restrictive policy on the handling of the Internet. It is a government-controlled Internet.

At least until very recently, in fact, when I was in Addis Ababa in July of last year, I tried to access my own blog at the Hilton Hotel, and I couldn't access it. I asked some of my Ethiopian friends, "What's going on here? I can't even get to my own blog." They just laughed, and said, "Oh, you didn't know that anything on blogspot is blocked in Ethiopia?" That is thanks to the technical assistance of the Chinese.

In the last several months, the counts on my blog suggest that Ethiopians are now accessing it. Something apparently has changed. But there has been some evidence of Chinese assisting certain governments in restricting information flow.

Senator CARDIN. Do you have any suggestions how the international community could try to counter those types of activities?

Ambassador SHINN. There probably are some technical ways to do it. I am just not knowledgeable about it. The only other way to approach it is simply continuing to raise these issues with China and with the African governments.

In the first instance, this is a problem for the African Governments because they are the ones that are authorizing these restrictive practices. I am sure we do have these talks with the Africans. I don't know whether we are having the discussions with the Chinese.

Senator CARDIN. And of course, it also says that we should be more aggressive in Africa. If we had more ties and there were more avenues for us to be able to exercise our influence, then we could have a better way of dealing with the type of relationships with China that are counterproductive with good governance.

Ambassador SHINN. I would certainly agree that we should be more aggressive in Africa, but not to the point where we are pushy. I think there is a fine line that one has to draw between being aggressive on policy and overstepping those bounds and looking like we are trying to boss everyone around.

Senator CARDIN. I agree with that, but we have had many hearings on this. But the United States, particularly in the AID programs, has to have a very strong position on anticorruption, women's rights, those issues. Because if not, then what do we stand for?

Ambassador SHINN. I would agree.

Senator CARDIN. Thank you.

Thank you, Mr. Chairman.

Senator COONS. Thank you, Senator Cardin.

Senator Lugar.

Senator LUGAR. Well, thank you very much, Mr. Chairman.

I thank you and Senator Isakson again for bringing about this hearing with three great witnesses. I think it is so important in terms of what you have pointed out subtly to all of us, which is that the degree of knowledge on the part of the Congress and our constituents about Africa certainly needs great improvement.

And the extent to which we have improvement with investment in Africa on the part of American businesses will largely come about because of support among the American business community for making the investments and taking the prudent risks, in addition to informed support from their stockholders and their constituencies. Transparency is important because people will say, "Why Africa? Why that market?"

And the fact is that we perhaps, as a nation, have not been as attentive or as competitive as we might be because we don't know a great deal about Africa. The basic facts of life about the 54 countries and much of the information you have given us today will be news to many people and, hopefully, will be conveyed by the media.

What I am hearing, however, and this oversimplifies, but we do have, as Senator Cardin was pointing out, very strong ideas, and they are good ones, about human rights and that we tend to approach foreign policy with these ideas in mind, and we should.

Now contrast that with the Chinese, who have a very business-like attitude. That their priority and continuity across the region hinges upon having energy resources in particular at this stage for their growth and the continued improvement of their material conditions.

Likewise, increasingly, we have reports about the amount of farming, agriculture and food literally coming out of Africa to feed the people of China. In other words, there are existential problems in China with regard to the continuity of their nation state. So, as a result, the Chinese may or may not care for any of the governments there, but these are the people with whom they do business.

Now we look at many of Africa's governments and we find corruption, lack of democracy, and what have you. Our tendency is to want to fix it, to try to move people and other resources around in response to the governance challenges, and remain much less attentive maybe to the business aspects of our bilateral relationships in Africa. I am not suggesting we follow the Chinese model, but currently the United States and China are carrying out two different policies on the same continent. And we should not be surprised, I think, at the testimony that you are giving.

What I am curious about down the trail, however, is, are there reasonable estimates as to how much oil and natural gas are in reserve in Africa? This is a great problem always asked around the world. And again and again, the time of reckoning is pushed back to a later date because more is found.

But I am curious literally as to what happens at the end of the trail when these resources diminish and become more dear, they are more expensive to whoever is going after them. Or as a matter of fact, in some African countries where they—if they are sufficiently developed—might have used some of these resources themselves, and this is no longer an option given inadequate technology or the premium on export.

Likewise, with agriculture, it would appear that we have been inhibited—that is, the United States—by European ideas on genetically modified seed, and therefore African countries still have very low production rates. Whatever the Chinese are taking out and whatever method they use notwithstanding, the fact is that Africans are going to find it increasingly difficult to feed themselves, quite apart from exporting to China.

Just from the standpoint of Africa, what are the mineral resources in reserve? Are they boundless? Does it depend upon the degree of development by a country, or how would you predict the future of these markets, however the United States or China approach them?

Dr. BRAUTIGAM. I will address part of that. I don't have data on the depth of resources in Africa, and I am not sure anyone does. What we do see is that as prices go up, more resources are found. And that has been the case for a long, long time.

And so, now we are finding all over West Africa and along the coast there, countries that never thought they had oil resources have suddenly found them. And of course, our companies are very active in that, and Chinese companies are trying to break into that without so far very much success.

I want to say something about agriculture. There is an idea that the Chinese are out there leading the land grab in Africa. It is one of the areas that I have been looking at at the International Food Policy Research Institute, where I am now.

And what we are finding is that there is actually no evidence of very large Chinese engagement in Africa to grow food to ship back to China at all. It doesn't exist, with the small exception of sesame seeds, which is not a vital resource.

There is some Chinese investment in agriculture for local consumption. In Zambia, there are some 25 Chinese farms that all produce for the Zambian market, but they are not yet doing speculative land investments. What we see is American and European firms that are active in land speculation.

And for investment in agriculture for feeding people at home, it is the Gulf States in the Arab world that are doing that and India, but not so far China.

So one other point about our different concerns about governance, and that is I think, as has come up in this hearing earlier, we both care about stability. That is very important. China's principles here are more consistent than ours are. And what China and many of its friends in Africa see is that the United States and Europe are engaging with China, and China is stable, but does not have a very good human rights record. And yet we are all there, investing and trading quite actively.

And China seems to be—the Chinese people seem to be doing better. They are becoming more prosperous. And so, that is something that is important for framing this conversation as well.

A small anecdote about Chinese engagement and governance. In Sierra Leone after the war, there was an election, and the presiding government lost. But they didn't want to give up power, for various reasons.

And a group of ambassadors went to talk to them, to the President, to say you have got to step down and let your opponent come in. And amongst that group of ambassadors was the Chinese Ambassador.

So I think this kind of engagement at the ambassadorial level is something we need to do a lot more of, and we are not doing enough of this in most of the countries that I am familiar with.

Thank you.

Mr. HAYES. I think, Senator, you are absolutely right in terms of the GMO issue. I think that is one of the really important issues that needs to be addressed, and the United States needs to press that more.

I also think that China is open to that. So there may be another area where China-United States could cooperate in breaking what I think is essentially a European blockade of American agriculture. I don't think there are many United States ag companies in Africa. I think that is a major problem. I also think it is a major opportunity for U.S. business.

I think there is enormous opportunity for agriculture and the United States, especially. We are still the leaders in the world in that area.

Senator LUGAR. And it will be an opportunity for Africans to have more food, likewise——

Mr. HAYES. Absolutely right.

Senator LUGAR. I thank you very much.

Ambassador SHINN. Senator, if I could just speak to the oil question? Ten percent of the world's oil reserves, known oil reserves, are in Africa. The experts think that as we look to the future, the continent that is going to come up with the largest percentage of new finds will be Africa because it has been relatively under-explored so far.

The experts also say that China's percent of oil imports is going to continue to grow at a significant rate. Now that may be because of increased demand. It may also be due to declining domestic production or a combination of both.

But those two trends suggest that the China-Africa oil link is going to become increasingly important in the years ahead.

Mr. HAYES. We are counting on 25 percent of our oil needs to be met by Africa by 2020. I think there is going to be an increasing and competitive environment, although, yes, there is more oil being discovered.

Senator COONS. Thank you, Senator Lugar.

Senator Durbin.

Senator DURBIN. Thank you, Mr. Chairman.

Last year I went to Ethiopia with Senator Sherrod Brown and met with Prime Minister Meles. We had a 30-minute meeting. And 25 minutes into the meeting, I asked Prime Minister Meles, "Oh, incidentally, what is the story about the presence of China in Ethiopia?" The meeting went on for 35 more minutes.

And basically, his message was pretty straightforward. "We think the United States has given up on Africa. China hasn't. China is investing in Africa in a way that nobody has ever seen before, and we have noticed it," he says, "in terms of the Chinese and their interest in our energy, our raw materials, our cheap labor, an opportunity for a growing middle class to buy their products."

And he said they come in with concessional loans many times, saying we will give you $100 million, just pay back $70 million for whatever the project is, so long as there are Chinese engineers, Chinese contractors, and half the workers are Chinese. And so, there is a pretty substantial presence of Chinese in Ethiopia and many other African countries. So they clearly have a plan, and they are executing it.

One European Foreign Minister told me, as I described this to him, he says, and there is one other factor you have missed. They will do business with anybody. The rules are very relaxed, as long as it meets their economic needs.

So what I put together here is a bill that Senator Coons has joined me on to talk about how we can improve our exports to Africa and our business in Africa and investments in Africa and try to coordinate this melange of agencies that we have that don't seem to work as well together as they should.

But as I listen to this hearing, I think the most significant thing that has come out of the hearing goes beyond what I have just said. And it started with Senator Coons's presentation with this chart behind me, which really tells a big story here about the fact that we are spending a significant amount of money in Africa for different things than the Chinese.

They are investing in infrastructure and building potential for economic growth. We are investing in people and health care.

So I asked my staff to take a look at the Global Fund. Most of us know the Global Fund. That is a group of nations around the world trying to find ways to alleviate human suffering from AIDS and malaria and tuberculosis all around the world.

In recent years, the United States has given $1 billion annually to the Global Fund. We are one of the largest donors. China, between 2003 and 2011, received $550 million from the Global Fund in grants. Another $200 million is pending. China's Global Fund contributions over recent years equaled $16 million, our contribution $5.5 billion.

So we are clearly putting money into Africa, and we have decided that we want to focus at least part of our commitment to Africa into alleviating human suffering and death. Zambia has been talked about a lot here. There is an interesting article in my notes given me about the recent election. And it became a backlash against the Chinese economic presence in Zambia.

And the Chinese Ambassador to Zambia ridiculed the writer, saying, "You send election judges. We build hospitals and roads in Zambia."

It turns out we spend $400 million a year in Zambia keeping 300,000 Zambians alive with antiretroviral drugs. So we are spending money there in different ways, and I guess virtue is going to have to be its own reward.

The last point I want to make before opening it up to your thoughts on this, every time you say "OECD," I kind of do the shorthand, which says no bribery. I think what you are suggesting is that if we could get China to play by some rules that we think we are playing by, we might have a better competitive situation with them. And if they are not going to play by those rules, we may not have as good a chance.

So how do you overcome this? We are not just strictly mercantile here. We are trying to alleviate human suffering and play by some rules on corruption and human rights. Do we have our hands tied behind our back, Ambassador Shinn?

Ambassador SHINN. Senator, you mentioned your meeting with Prime Minister Meles—I have had similar conversations with him as recently as several years ago.

Ethiopia is one of the major recipients of the Global Fund. It is also one of the major recipients of bilateral HIV/AIDS support from the U.S. Government. The problem is that HIV/AIDS money and emergency food aid probably accounts for two-thirds of all American assistance to Africa today. It is taken for granted by the Africans. We just don't get the credit for it that we deserve, quite frankly.

The Chinese go in with a loan that has to be paid back, albeit it is concessionary financing, build a road or a dam or a bridge. All of a sudden, it becomes the Chinese road or the Chinese dam or the Chinese bridge, and everyone in the vicinity knows about it. So China gets all sorts of credit for that. It is very smart on China's part to do that.

It puts us in a very difficult position because we are simply not getting the credit that we rightly deserve, even from someone as sophisticated as Prime Minister Meles. He knows the numbers. He knows them better than anyone in this room.

But I don't know how you deal with that issue. It may just be the nature of the beast.

I would like to make a pitch for one organization, though, that hasn't yet been mentioned in terms of what the U.S. Government can do, and that is support for the Overseas Private Investment Corporation. It is very small organization. I used to deal with it when I was Ambassador, and I found it to be an effective organization in what it did. But it is very small.

Senator DURBIN. Mr. Hayes, you said we should be shifting USAID toward the private sector. That seems to say to me spend less on health care, spend less on educating young women, more on establishing mercantile, business relationships.

Mr. HAYES. Well, I think that we have got to look at a greater balance certainly in aid and how we use that, and also there are other ways beyond simply money, in terms of training, capacity-building, and so forth. So I think, yes, I do say that we need to put more emphasis on building a middle class because then I think it makes the other money that we are spending less needed ultimately.

Senator DURBIN. These are Faustian choices, 300,000 people living——

Mr. HAYES. Indeed, they are.

Senator DURBIN [continuing]. With HIV retroviral drugs who would be, some of them, cut off in the name of establishing a better business relationship.

Mr. HAYES. I am not convinced that it is an either/or choice. I think that——

Senator DURBIN. With this budget, it is.

Mr. HAYES. I think the issues of commercial offices, stronger commercial presence. For God's sake, send the Secretary of Commerce to Africa once every 10 years.

Senator DURBIN. We now have one.

Mr. HAYES. It has been 10 years since the last Secretary of Commerce visited. There are other ways to develop those ties. I——

Senator DURBIN. I am sorry.

Mr. HAYES. Go ahead.

Senator DURBIN. Dr. Brautigam, I want to give you one last word, if you would like?

Dr. BRAUTIGAM. I think, ultimately, Africans are going to have to pay for their own health care in the long term. And how are they going to have the foundation to do that? They are going to have to build up their business sectors. They are going to have to be able to tax, and they are going to have to be able to get the revenues.

And I think the Chinese approach—looking at the infrastructure, looking at business engagement—is moving toward that kind of future. Whereas our approach, which is laudable in many ways, the amount of money that we are putting into health care in Africa, we are keeping a lot more people alive, but we aren't doing much about providing jobs for them.

Senator COONS. Thank you, Senator Durbin.

Our last questions today will come from Senator Udall.

43

Senator UDALL. Thank you, Chairman Coons, and thank you both for holding this important hearing.

I wanted to focus a little bit on—and I think it was very important we got into the human rights issues and corruption and all the issues that Senator Durbin just raised. I wanted to focus a little bit on environmental issues.

You mentioned, Profession Shinn, in your testimony that China has four hard interests in Africa. And you mentioned as one of those—on one of the four—energy, minerals, timber, and agriculture products. And obviously, if you are talking about—we would like to see, I would assume our policy is sustainable economic development.

That we do these things—you can develop energy and minerals and timber and agriculture in such a way that you do it sustainably. That you do it where you don't harm the environment, where—you mentioned dams, you build dams in such a way that you don't dislocate local people.

I know there is a dam that has been mentioned here recently in the news that the Chinese are funding, where 300,000 Kenyans would be deprived of their water needed for agriculture, cattle herding, and fishing.

And so, the real—my question is looking at how Western countries, and mainly the Western developed countries, participate in Africa and how their practices compare with the Chinese and what you see there. What are the things that we can do about if there is a disparity and they are not practicing sustainable practices, then what can we do to try to encourage them to do so?

And the other witnesses also may have comments on this. So, please, why don't you lead off?

Ambassador SHINN. Thank you, Senator. That is an interesting question, and it is also a very timely one.

If you were to go back 5 or 6 years and look at Chinese projects in Africa and the environmental consequences of those projects, you would have a fair amount to criticize. There was, for example, a plan to develop iron ore in Gabon. The problem was that in order to do so, China would have to rip up a local game park in order to implement that project.

There was so much opposition from both local environmental groups and international environmental groups that the whole thing was scrubbed, and it is being revisited in terms of how the project moves forward.

China does not have a great record, obviously, on environmental issues. Western projects, I think, across the board must have environmental impact assessments. It is certainly true in the case of American projects and, I think, most Western governments. That has traditionally not been the case with many of the Chinese projects.

But, and this is a good news story. I think you are starting to see a change in the Chinese approach to how they deal environmentally not only with their projects overseas, but what is happening in China. I think the Three Gorges Dam has been a real wakeup call for them. They are now seeing some very negative environmental impacts from the construction of that project, and it is causing them to rethink how they deal with the environment in

China. That is impacting how they deal with projects outside of China.

You are hearing more and more about Chinese actually employing outside Western companies to do environmental impact statements for their projects, and that, I think, would have been unheard of 5 or 6 years ago.

Senator UDALL. You see that as a real improvement for them, weighing in on these issues of how you balance sustainability and still get what you need for your country?

Ambassador SHINN. I do see it as an improvement, but China is still well behind Western countries and getting to the point where it needs to be. But the trend is in the right direction.

Senator UDALL. And is there more that we can do to encourage them to do this kind of thing?

Ambassador SHINN. I don't have any ideas other than having these conversations at senior levels with appropriate Chinese officials and also with the African officials who are signing these agreements with China. They need to understand that there has to be an environmental impact statement and assessment before you go ahead with a project.

And I think that is what is happening with this Gibe III Dam project in Ethiopia that impacts Lake Turkana in Kenya. I think that is the project you were referring to.

Senator UDALL. That is the one I was referring to.

Ambassador SHINN. Gibe III has raised a firestorm of difficulties among the Kenyans and even among some Ethiopians who would be displaced as a result of construction of the dam.

On the other hand, the region desperately needs more hydropower. So there have to be some offsets there. But better environmental studies are clearly needed by the African countries and in terms of the Chinese who are doing a lot of these projects.

Senator UDALL. Dr. Brautigam.

Dr. BRAUTIGAM. I would agree with Ambassador Shinn's assessment of the changes that we have seen happening with Chinese financiers. They are very interested in corporate social responsibility as a concept. Adopting these kinds of practices is still going to take quite a while, though. It took us a while to get there.

I was young when the World Bank was the big problem actor in this regard, funding these kinds of projects overseas. And eventually, they changed. And the Chinese will probably change in the future, and we can see signs of that already.

But the way this change happens is in part through pressure from outside, and it comes from a lot of different players—from the U.S. Treasury Department, from civil society, and from informed analysis. But I think the pressure is not coming from African governments.

And the Chinese standards, surprisingly, for environmental assessment are higher in China than they are in most parts of Africa. And so, that is part of the challenge now that we have a new actor here. Whose standards will prevail?

But we can see this change amongst the Chinese in other areas as well. Few people realize this, but the Chinese have actually made overseas bribery into a crime in China. So that was never the case before. This just happened very recently. It is part of their responsibilities under their signing of the U.N. convention against corruption.

They don't yet have good enforcement for that, and it is very new. And we know a lot of our partners in Europe aren't enforcing this very well, either. But this is a change, and these are the kinds of things that we can see signs of. And it is up to us to know about those and then to encourage them.

Senator UDALL. Great. Mr. Hayes, do you have any thoughts on this or——

Mr. HAYES. Well, I have thoughts, but it is not too different from what you have already heard from the two witnesses. I think our diplomacy, particularly with the African Governments in this case, needs to be strengthened.

Senator UDALL. The one thing I would note and then turn my time back here is that apparently—and Dr. Shinn, correct me if I am wrong. But I think China ignored the EIS from the World Bank in the Gibe III case, having to do with the dam? Is that correct that there was an EIS? It was done by the World Bank and that they just went ahead. I don't know if they have made adjustments.

Ambassador SHINN. I don't know the answer to that, whether they did or not.

Senator UDALL. OK.

Ambassador SHINN. It would be better not to comment on, as I just don't know.

Senator UDALL. OK. OK. Well, as you noted, I mean, this is a— I have a report here that says, you know, this Omo River is responsible for 90 percent of the water heading into Lake Turkana. A major dam blocking the river would drain most of the lake, depriving 300,000 Kenyans of the water needed for agriculture, cattle herding, fishing, and this Omo River could affect—the changes in it that we are talking about, and I think that you mentioned, could affect 70 percent or more of an important species around the lake. So, you know, that is major damage being done by a major part of their effort in terms of their loan that they put out there.

So, thank you, Mr. Chairman. Really appreciate you holding this hearing.

Senator COONS. Thank you, Senator Udall.

Unfortunately, we have reached 3:30 p.m., and as I shared with the panel before we began, we have a briefing to which all Senators need to turn now.

I just want to thank you very much for sharing your insights and your expertise on these critically important subjects that have significant implications for the economic and political future of the United States, of China, and of the people of Africa.

There are so many remaining interesting questions I would like to have gotten into about intellectual property protection, the role of the other BRIC nations, multilateral means for more effectively engaging with China, and ways to develop shared standards for everything from labor protections to environmental protections, to advancing human rights, and then ways to diversify the economic opportunities of Africans going forward. But we will have to wait for some future opportunity.

With that, I will conclude today's meeting. I thank the witnesses, and we will keep the record open for any Senators to submit statements for the record until the close of business Thursday, November 3.

Senator COONS. Thank you very much.

This hearing is hereby concluded.

[Whereupon, at 3:30 p.m., the hearing was adjourned.]

○